WASHINGTON, D.C.
PAST AND PRESENT

WASHINGTON, D.C.

PAST AND PRESENT

PETER R. PENCZER

ONEONTA PRESS

This book is dedicated to Madeline Li and my parents, Peter and Lynne Penczer, without whose unwavering support this book would not have been possible.

Copyright © 1998 by Peter R. Penczer

All rights reserved

Printed in the United States of America

Oneonta Press
5519 N. 22nd Street
Arlington, VA 22205

Washington, D.C., Past and Present

ISBN 0-9629841-1-6

Library of Congress Catalog Card Number: 98-91447

Frontispiece: The Baltimore and Potomac Railroad Station on B Street (now Constitution Avenue) at Sixth Street, November, 1906

Cover Design: Margött Weltin

CONTENTS

ACKNOWLEDGMENTS   6

INTRODUCTION   7

MAPS   8

THE MALL   10

CAPITOL HILL   44

THE WHITE HOUSE   52

PENNSYLVANIA AVENUE   54

FEDERAL TRIANGLE   68

JUDICIARY SQUARE   76

DOWNTOWN   78

MIDTOWN   118

NORTHWEST   132

NORTHEAST   154

FOGGY BOTTOM   158

SOUTHWEST   160

SOUTHEAST   172

GEORGETOWN   178

ARLINGTON COUNTY   198

FALLS CHURCH   216

FAIRFAX COUNTY   220

ALEXANDRIA   230

MONTGOMERY COUNTY   240

PRINCE GEORGES COUNTY   256

PHOTOGRAPH CREDITS   264

ACKNOWLEDGMENTS

Many individuals assisted with the preparation of this book, but I would especially like to thank Anne Whitmore, for her diligent and thoughtful editing of the manuscript; Margött Weltin, for the countless hours she spent designing the cover; Madeline Li, for her keen editorial eye; and Paul Gillis, for the generous use of his photographic equipment. My thanks go also to Robert A. Truax, who shared his knowledge of Washington history and generously lent maps and photographs from his collection for use in this work, and James M. Goode, for his many helpful suggestions. Of the numerous archivists and librarians who assisted me, I am especially grateful to Matthew Gilmore and Mary Ternes of the Washingtoniana Division of the D.C. Public Library, Cindy Janke of the Kiplinger Washington Collection, Sam Daniel of the Prints and Photographs Division of the Library of Congress, and Jim Palmer of the Arlington Historical Society. Cindy Janke, Robert A. Truax, and Frank Wright reviewed the completed manuscript prior to publication, and I thank them for their invaluable comments and suggestions. I would like to acknowledge the generosity of all those who provided access to rooftops around the city, with a special thank you to Stephanie Barrett of the Melwood Apartments. Finally, I would like to express my gratitude to the photographers who took the vintage photographs that appear here, most of whom remain anonymous. Their contribution towards preserving the history of our city has been incalculable. By name I would like to thank Joseph Owen Curtis, whose work appears on pages 162 and 166, and John P. Wymer, whose work appears on pages 126, 140, 148, and 158.

INTRODUCTION

The earliest extant photographs of Washington, D.C., are a small set of daguerreotypes dating from about 1846. The work of John Plumbe, Jr., they depict the most important Washington landmarks: the Capitol, the White House, the Patent Office, and the old General Post Office Building. Each of these landmarks is standing today, and in this Washington is fortunate.

Of course, the city has changed immensely in many other ways. The federal-style houses that once lined Pennsylvania Avenue and the streets downtown have all but disappeared. The elaborate commercial buildings that replaced them in the late nineteenth century have themselves been replaced by modern office buildings built in glass and concrete.

The great engine of change in Washington has been the expansion of the federal government. In Plumbe's day, there were only 1,500 federal employees in Washington, and the city had barely 50,000 inhabitants. Washington was a compact city. The built-up area extended only as far north as K Street, and most Washingtonians walked to work. Today over four million persons live in the metropolitan area.

With the introduction of electric streetcars, around 1890, it became practical for Washingtonians to commute to their jobs in the city. Real estate developers bought large tracts of land in the country, subdivided them into lots, and built trolley lines connecting them to the city. The new streetcar suburbs were located within the District and without, and their names are familiar today: Cleveland Park, Brookland, Chevy Chase, Takoma Park, Clarendon, and many others.

Beginning in the 1920s, the widespread availability of the automobile again changed the face of metropolitan Washington. Fueled by the expansion of the federal workforce during Franklin Roosevelt's New Deal and World War II, the empty spaces between and beyond the streetcar lines filled with suburbs. Shoppers patronized the new stores in the suburbs, and the commercial area downtown, once the site of most retail business in the metropolitan area, withered and died.

Meanwhile, the city's monumental core was transformed in a more direct fashion by the federal government. In the late nineteenth century, the mud flats of the Potomac were dredged and converted to landfill, adding over 600 acres to the city, and the Washington Monument, abandoned in an unfinished state for more than twenty years, was completed. In 1902, the Senate Park Commission Plan laid out a road map for the future development of the Mall, envisioning rows of gleaming white buildings surrounded by orderly parks. Over the decades that followed, acres of buildings were cleared, and the Lincoln Memorial, Reflecting Pool, and Memorial Bridge were built.

In the 1930s, the blighted triangle between the Mall and Pennsylvania Avenue was razed and rebuilt with classically styled federal office buildings. In the 1950s and 1960s, Southwest Washington, between the Mall and the Potomac, was demolished and rebuilt in a massive urban renewal project. In the 1980s, Pennsylvania Avenue was rehabilitated by the Pennsylvania Avenue Development Corporation, a federal agency.

I hope that every reader will be able to find among these 127 pairs of photographs many familiar places and be surprised by how much, and in some cases how little, the city has changed. At the same time, I hope that readers will gain a better appreciation for the forces that have changed the physical appearance of the city so dramatically.

For each of the 127 vintage photographs in this book, I have taken great pains to ensure that the recent view was taken from exactly the same camera position. There are many fine early photographs of Washington that I was not able to use because the vantage point is no longer accessible or could not be accurately located. In some cases the vantage point of the early photograph was easy to determine, particularly where many of the older buildings were still standing. In other cases, where the landscape has changed entirely, such as Tysons Corner, it was quite difficult. After processing, each of the photographs was digitized and I used a computer to match and crop each of the 127 pairs.

About half of the recent photographs were taken with a Sinar F view camera equipped with Schneider lenses, on 4-by-5-inch sheet film. Many of the photographs were taken in busy streets by hastily setting up and removing my camera as traffic permitted. In such cases, using the cumbersome view camera would have been impossible and instead I used a Nikon FE2 with a 35mm PC-Nikkor or one of several other lenses. At times I used an Olympus OM-1 and OM-2n with 28mm and 50mm lenses. About ten of the recent photographs were taken with medium format cameras, either a Pentax 6x7 or a Mamiya M645. I used Kodak black-and-white film, principally TRI-X, T-MAX, and Technical Pan.

The preparation of *Washington, D.C., Past and Present* was a very rewarding and educational process. I never lost a sense of wonder over the power of time to change our physical environment. I hope that the reader enjoys reading this work as much as I enjoyed writing it.

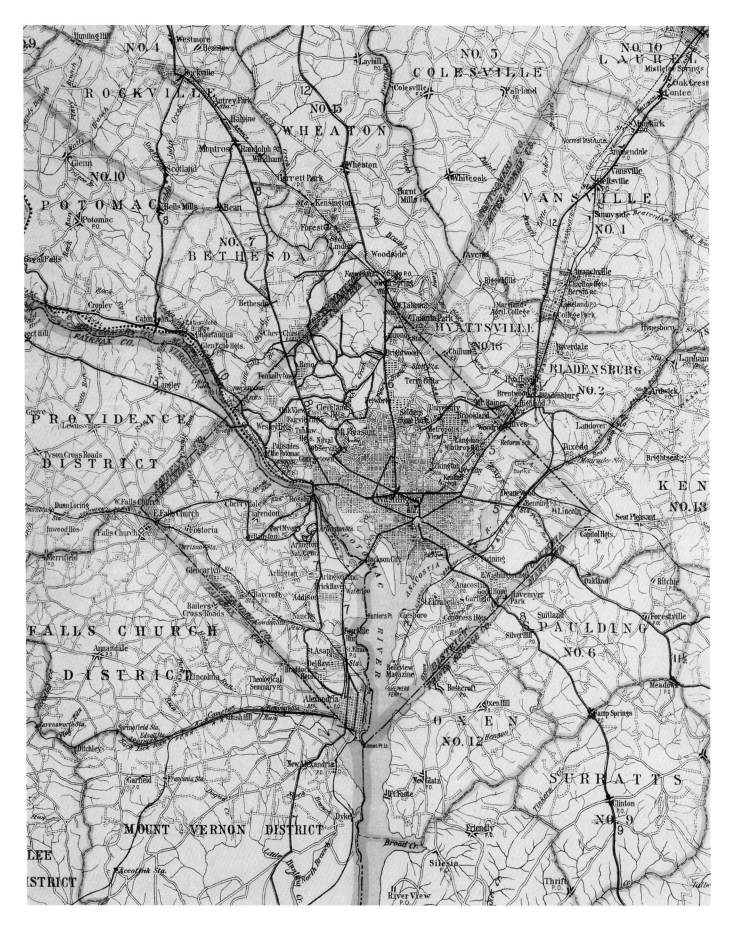

Automobile Map of Washington District, Walker Lith. & Pub. Co., Boston, 1909 (detail)

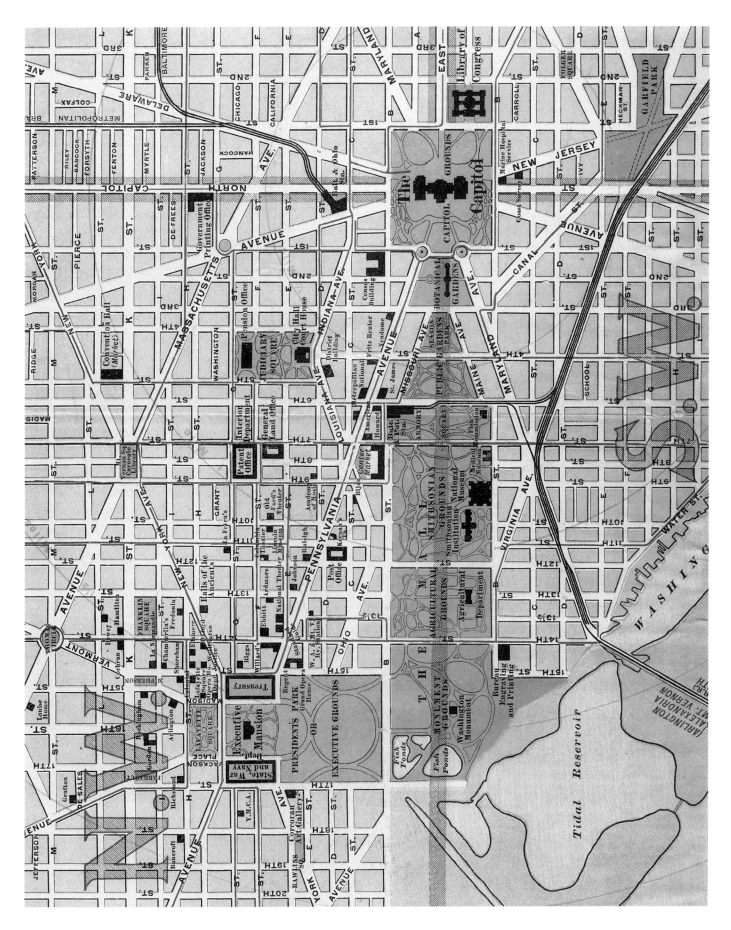

"Standard Guide" Ready Reference Map of Washington, Foster & Reynolds, Washington, 1901 (detail)

1911

Looking east from the Washington Monument. The newly constructed United States National Museum, now the National Museum of Natural History, stands almost alone on the Mall in the view below. Directly opposite the museum is the castle-like Smithsonian Building, completed in the 1850s. The Mall is covered with trees and winding paths—a naturalistic landscaping plan that pre-dated the Civil War. In the 1930s, a more formal and rectilinear scheme was adopted that was thought to be more in keeping with the original intentions of the city's designer, Pierre Charles L'Enfant. Museums have since filled in most of the available space on the Mall. In the lower left corner of the recent photograph is the National Museum of American History, finished in 1964. Beyond the Natural History Museum on the north (left) side of the Mall is the domed West Building of the National Gallery of Art and the geometric East Building. Across the Mall, beyond the Smithsonian "Castle," is the Smithsonian's Arts and Industries Building, the cylindrical Hirshhorn Museum, and the National Air and Space Museum.

24 October 1995

c. 1904

Looking north from the Washington Monument. The White House and its grounds look relatively unchanged in these two photographs, taken ninety-odd years apart. On the left in both views is the Old Executive Office Building, built in stages in the 1870s and 1880s. Derided for many years as an architectural monstrosity, the enormous empire-style building survived several attempts to remodel it to match the Treasury Building on the opposite side of the White House. Midtown Washington fills the area beyond the White House in both views. At the turn of the century it was a genteel residential area, but today it is solidly occupied by office buildings.

25 October 1995

c. 1902

Looking northeast from the Washington Monument. Federal Triangle, now filled with monumental federal office buildings, was as late as 1930 a rather motley industrial area. The power plant, with its large smokestack, was only about five years old when the photograph below was taken around 1902. It was demolished in 1930 to make way for construction of the building that now houses the United States Customs Service. To the left in the recent view is the enormous Department of Commerce Building, the largest office building in the nation when it was completed in 1932. At the far right in both views is the Old Post Office Building, with its tall tower and clock. Built in 1899 in the Romanesque Revival style, it clashed with its more classical neighbors when the Federal Triangle project was built in the 1930s. Narrowly escaping demolition, the building was restored in the early 1980s and opened to the public as a shopping mall. The upper floors house government offices.

24 October 1995

1911

Looking northwest from the Washington Monument. A naked-looking Constitution Avenue runs past the border of Foggy Bottom in the photograph below. In the lower right, at the corner of Constitution Avenue and Seventeenth Street, is the newly constructed home of the Pan-American Union, now the Organization of American States. The area in the lower left was once part of the Potomac River and had been filled in at the end of the nineteenth century. Today it is the site of a six-acre artificial lake. Across Constitution Avenue, in the center of the photograph, the land was largely vacant, because poor drainage left it somewhat swampy. Constitution Avenue itself had been the site of a canal until the early 1870s, when the waterway was filled in. The presence of the canal and the proximity of the river attracted industry to Foggy Bottom in the early years of the capital, and the area retained its industrial character until at least the 1930s. The vacant land in the foreground would soon be filled with temporary buildings constructed during World War I as offices for government workers. Later, beginning in the 1930s, larger and more permanent office buildings filled Foggy Bottom. Just beyond the O.A.S. Building in the recent view is the massive Interior Department Building, with its six identical wings, completed in 1936.

015676 WASHINGTON FROM THE MONUMENT.

25 October 1995

1911

Looking southeast from the Washington Monument. Incredible as it may seem, virtually every one of the buildings in the photograph below was demolished in a series of federal projects between 1930 and 1960. Thousands of houses, apartment buildings, churches, and businesses—entire neighborhoods—disappeared. In the 1930s government office buildings began to encroach on the area from Independence Avenue (foreground, running diagonally). Completed in 1937 was the massive South Building of the Department of Agriculture, which fills the foreground in the recent view. Two bridges connect it with older Agriculture buildings across Independence Avenue. The avenue itself was widened in 1941, necessitating the destruction of two churches and dozens of homes. Then, in the 1950s, 550 acres were razed as part of an urban renewal project. In the 1960s the area was rebuilt; many of the large buildings in the center of the recent photograph date from that period. Beyond them lie the apartment buildings and townhouses that replaced some of the thousands of modest, and in many cases dilapidated, homes that were demolished.

24 October 1995

1918

Looking south from the Washington Monument towards East Potomac Park. In the center of both views is East Potomac Park, an artificial island formed when mud flats were dredged at the end of the nineteenth century. Surrounding the park is the Washington Channel (left), the Tidal Basin (right foreground), and the Potomac River (rear). In the earlier view, a bathing beach can be seen on banks of the Tidal Basin. It was later the site of the Jefferson Memorial, dedicated in 1943. Just beyond the memorial is the Potomac Railroad Bridge, built in 1901. It is still in use, but the overhead trusses have been removed. Today it is joined by a bridge for Metrorail trains and the three spans of the Fourteenth Street Bridge, one of which is visible in the photograph to the right.

25 October 1995

18 August 1863

Looking east from the Smithsonian Building. The photograph below and the three Civil War–era views on the following pages were taken by Titian Ramsay Peale from the tallest tower of the Smithsonian "Castle." In this view, looking east, the almost-finished dome of the Capitol can be seen on the horizon. At the start of the war, soldiers were lodged in the rotunda beneath the great dome and bread for the troops was baked in the basement. Later, the Capitol served as a hospital for the wounded. The square building in the right center is the Washington Armory, built in 1855 to house the weapons of the District militia. During the Civil War, the armory became the Armory Square Hospital. In the view below, the wooden buildings and numerous tents of the hospital are arrayed across the Mall from the armory on the right to the Washington Canal on the left. The building served a number of purposes until it was demolished in 1964, and today the site is occupied by the National Air and Space Museum.

27 February 1996

18 October 1863

Looking north from the Smithsonian Building. A naturalistic landscaping scheme decorated the Mall around the Smithsonian Building during the second half of the nineteenth century; its trees and winding paths can be seen below. Bordering the Mall on the north is the Washington Canal, opened in 1815 and filled in in the 1870s. Crossing the canal is a bridge that provided access to the Smithsonian from Tenth Street. The area beyond the canal, today's Federal Triangle, was prone to flooding and relegated to marginal uses. During the Civil War it housed a notorious red light district known as "Hooker's Division." Soldiers came here to visit the many brothels, gamble, or lose their money to the pickpockets and swindlers. In the recent view, Constitution Avenue has replaced the canal, but it is completely obscured in the photograph by the National Museum of Natural History, completed in 1911. Beyond the museum are the massive buildings of Federal Triangle. On the left is the tower of the Old Post Office Building. It stands on Pennsylvania Avenue and marks the northern limit of Federal Triangle.

27 February 1996

18 October 1863

Looking west from the Smithsonian Building. In the center of the view below is the unfinished stump of the Washington Monument. At the time of the Civil War, the area around the base was used as a depot for cattle destined to feed the troops. Almost lapping at the base of the monument are the waters of the Potomac. In the river beyond the monument are mud flats, and on the extreme right is the mouth of the Washington Canal. Landfill operations commenced in the 1870s and lasted until 1913; more than 600 acres were added to the city. On the left in the present view is the Department of Agriculture. It is the only building on the Mall that is not open to the public. Beyond the Washington Monument is the Lincoln Memorial, dedicated in 1922.

27 February 1996

27 February 1996

18 October 1863

Looking south from the Smithsonian Building. The area around Tenth Street, in the southwest quadrant of the city, has changed dramatically since the Civil War. Only the crenelated tower of the Smithsonian "Castle" in the bottom center of each view, and the Maryland and Virginia hills on the horizon form a common frame of reference. Even the Potomac has been partially filled by East Potomac Park. In the foreground is Independence Avenue, since widened. Beyond it in the earlier view is Virginia Avenue, running diagonally. Urban renewal transformed the area in the 1950s and 1960s, and this section

of Virginia Avenue has disappeared. In the center of the early view is Tenth Street, leading from Independence Avenue to the waterfront. Today it is spanned by the Forrestal Building, set on 36-foot pillars. In the 1960s Tenth Street was intended to be the gateway and centerpiece of the newly redeveloped Southwest Washington; it would lead from Independence Avenue to a cultural center at its far end. Instead, the cultural center was built in Foggy Bottom (as the Kennedy Center), and today Tenth Street leads nowhere.

27 February 1996

c. 1885

Looking southeast from the Smithsonian Building. This view was taken from the same vantage point as the four Civil War–era views on the preceding pages, but it postdates them by about twenty years. In the foreground is the roof of the Smithsonian's Arts and Industries Building, completed in 1881 to house exhibits from the 1876 Centennial Exposition in Philadelphia. Just beyond it in the recent view is the 231-foot cylinder of the Hirshhorn Museum, which houses a collection of contemporary art given to the nation by Joseph H. Hirshhorn. The building was completed in 1974. On the extreme left in the recent photograph is the National Air and Space Museum. It opened in 1976 and has since become the most-visited museum in the world. On the right, facing Independence Avenue, is a federal office building. Such structures have spread southward from the Mall, replacing the rowhouses and modest commercial structures of the previous century.

27 February 1996

c. 1930

Looking northwest towards the 100 block of Pennsylvania Avenue from the Peace Monument. This block of souvenir shops and lunch rooms stood directly across the street from the Capitol. The block was cleared around 1933 in accordance with the 1902 Senate Park Commission Plan, better known as the McMillan Plan. A guide for the development of the capital city, the plan envisioned rows of gleaming white buildings along the Mall surrounded by orderly, rectilinear landscaping. The reality in 1902 was quite different—commercial and residential structures, government buildings, and a train station encroached upon the Mall in a haphazard fashion. Over the following decades, work proceeded slowly, but many aspects of the plan were implemented. Many blocks were cleared and landscaped, and the Lincoln Memorial, the Reflecting Pool, and the Memorial Bridge, all foreseen by the McMillan Plan, were built. On the far left in the present view is the tower of the Old Post Office Building, far down Pennsylvania Avenue. On the right is the massive Department of Labor Building.

16 March 1997

c. 1930

Looking northwest towards the corner of Missouri Avenue and Third Street. This block of venerable old homes stood on the Mall until around 1930, when it was cleared, in keeping with the 1902 Senate Park Commission Plan. Third Street, in the foreground, still crosses the Mall, but Missouri Avenue, on the left in the earlier view, has disappeared entirely. The name "Missouri Avenue" has since been reassigned to another street, in Northwest Washington. The site stood vacant for many years until the construction of the East Building of the National Gallery of Art. Designed by I. M. Pei and completed in 1978, the East Building is considered by many to be the finest work of modern architecture in the city.

1 February 1997

November 1906

Sixth Street looking south towards the intersection with B Street (now Constitution Avenue). The Baltimore and Potomac Railroad Station, pictured below, was the first target of the Senate Park Commission. For decades after its construction in 1873, the station was an eyesore. Its train sheds extended into the Mall, and smoke-belching steam trains chugged on rails stretching across the formal park. President James A. Garfield was assassinated here on July 2, 1881, shot in the back by Charles Guiteau, a deranged self-taught lawyer who had hoped to be appointed Ambassador to Paris. The President died two months later of his wound, and Guiteau was hanged in the old D.C. jail. The station was demolished in 1907, replaced by Union Station, so named because it unified rail service to Washington into one station (Union Station also served the Baltimore and Ohio Railroad, whose station on nearby New Jersey Avenue was razed the same year). Sixth Street no longer crosses the Mall, and today the West Building of the National Gallery of Art, completed in 1941, occupies the site.

12 September 1995

15 July 1941

Independence Avenue, S.W., looking west from Seventh Street. Independence Avenue, today a major thoroughfare, was once just wide enough for two cars to pass. This photograph was taken by the *Evening Star* to document the appearance of the avenue before its widening in 1941 forced the removal of two churches, dozens of homes, and many shade trees on the south (left) side of the street. The building on the right is the Army Medical Museum, built in 1887. It was demolished in 1969 for the construction of the Hirshhorn Museum, despite its designation as a National Historic Landmark. Today the museum, now the National Museum of Health and Medicine, is housed on the grounds of the Walter Reed Army Medical Center on Georgia Avenue.

30 September 1995

14 August 1879

The Washington Monument. When this photograph was taken in 1879, work had just resumed on the Washington Monument after a hiatus of more than twenty years. Work was originally undertaken by the Washington Monument Society, with funds donated by the public. The cornerstone was laid in 1848, and construction proceeded slowly. In 1855 control of the society was seized by the Know-Nothings, a nativist political party, after the Pope donated a memorial stone to the monument. The group dumped the stone into the Potomac and work stalled that year at the 156-foot level. The monument remained an unsightly stump until 1876, when Congress undertook its completion. Engineers found

29 October 1995

that the original stone base was inadequate, given the monument's location on soft, sandy soil at the edge of the Potomac. In the earlier photograph preparations are being made for concrete reinforcements. Work proceeded rapidly, and the monument was dedicated in 1885. At its completion, the Washington Monument was the tallest building in the world, but five years later it was surpassed in height by the Eiffel Tower. It remains the world's tallest masonry structure. The stone used to complete the monument was slightly different in color from that used in the original section pictured to the left, and the difference can be detected in the recent photograph.

c. 1895

The lockkeeper's house on the southwest corner of B Street (now Constitution Avenue) and Seventeenth Street. It is difficult to imagine today, but this building, constructed here around 1835, once stood at the edge of the Potomac River, now two-thirds of a mile distant. It served as a lockkeeper's house on an extension of the Chesapeake and Ohio Canal, which ran from the mouth of Rock Creek, along the Potomac, and down the length of present-day Constitution Avenue (from the right in the photographs) to this spot. Here it passed through a lock and into the mouth of the Washington Canal on the Potomac River. The lockkeeper's house was built on a spit of land between the canal and the river, and the waters of the Potomac reached almost to the back of the house. By the time the photograph below was taken, the canal was long gone and the river behind the house had been reclaimed by landfill. Landscaping on this part of the Mall was still years away, and the house appears to have been occupied by squatters. The building later served as a public restroom, and today it is vacant.

29 June 1996

c. 1846

East front of the United States Capitol. This extraordinary daguerreotype of the Capitol was bought for a few dollars in a flea market in Alameda, California, in 1971, and shortly thereafter sold to the Library of Congress. A similar image by the same photographer, John Plumbe Jr., sold in 1995 for $170,000. All told, there are eight surviving period daguerreotypes of Washington subjects, seven by Plumbe. This one is particularly important because it depicts the Capitol as it appeared between 1829 and 1851, before the present dome and wings were added. On the right is the old Senate wing, first occupied in 1800 when Congress moved from Philadelphia to Washington. Its cornerstone was set in 1793 by George Washington himself, and the wing stood alone until the corresponding House wing was completed in 1807. The two wings were

30 March 1997

connected by a wooden walkway when the entire structure was torched by the British in August 1814. The interior was largely gutted in the fire but the exterior walls survived. The wings were soon rebuilt, and work started on the center section in 1818 under the direction of Charles Bullfinch. An inner dome was made of masonry, while the outer dome was wood covered in copper. Work was not completed until 1829. Although they appear to be identical, the portico and walls visible in the recent photograph are not the same as those in the daguerreotype. Between 1959 and 1961, the east front was extended outward 32½ feet; a replica portico and walls were built in marble and the original walls were buried in the new structure. The sandstone columns dating from Bullfinch's time are now standing at the National Arboretum on New York Avenue.

8 January 1858

West front of the United States Capitol. By 1850, the size of Congress had more than doubled and the building depicted in the Plumbe daguerreotype was becoming a bit cramped. That year, Congress appropriated money for additions that would almost triple the size of the Capitol. The following year, work began on two new wings for the House and Senate. By 1855, it was clear that the greatly enlarged Capitol would dwarf Bulfinch's wooden dome, and Congress authorized construction of a new and larger dome. In the photograph below, taken in 1858, the dome can be seen under construction; it is built of iron painted white to match the rest of the structure. The House wing, on the far right, not yet finished, was occupied for the first

25 March 1996

time a few weeks earlier. On the far left is the new Senate wing, under construction and not occupied until the following year. In the foreground is the Washington Canal, opened in 1815. It ran down Constitution Avenue, in front of the Capitol, and on to the Anacostia River. Canal boats, at least in plan, moved cargo between the then deep-water Anacostia River (known as the Eastern Branch in those days) and the Chesapeake and Ohio Canal, avoiding the currents of the Potomac. Early prints depicted the canal as a beautiful grand canal worthy of Venice; in fact it was a malodorous open sewer. Constant silting left this section in front of the Capitol hardly useable for much of its life, and the entire canal was filled in in the early 1870s.

18 December 1895

Looking south from the steps of the Library of Congress towards B Street (now Independence Avenue), S.E. Finishing touches are being made to the exterior of the new Library of Congress: tiles are being laid on the front terrace, which today seems remarkably unchanged in the century that has passed. Less than two years later, in 1897, the imposing edifice was opened to the public. In the background is a row of nine-teenth-century structures fronting on Independence Avenue. In the 1950s there were quite a few restaurants here and the strip was known as Ptomaine Row. The block was razed in 1962 and stood empty for almost a decade. By 1971, work was underway on the present Madison Building, an annex to the

31 March 1996

Library of Congress. The building's architecture was widely criticized as sterile and unimaginative, and a *Washington Post* critic compared it to the work of Nazi architect Albert Speer. On the right in the recent photograph is the Cannon House Office Building, constructed at the same time as the Russell Senate Office Building. Completed in 1908, the two buildings provided the first official office space outside of the Capitol for members of Congress. Previously, many members had rented space in downtown Washington.

c. 1890

New Jersey Avenue, S.E., looking northwest towards B Street (now Independence Avenue) and the Capitol. The light-colored building on the corner was constructed in 1874 by Benjamin Butler, Massachusetts congressman and Civil War general. The house contained two large townhouses, which Butler rented out; President Chester Arthur lived in the corner unit during renovations to the White House. Butler died in 1893 and the house was taken over by the United States Coast and Geodetic Survey, which occupied the imposing brick structure to the left. The Butler house was demolished in 1929 for construction of the Longworth House Office Building, completed in 1933.

5 April 1996

c. 1861

North front of the White House. This is the White House as Lincoln saw it, with gas lamps mounted on the columns of the portico and a statue of Thomas Jefferson on the lawn. James Hoban designed the building, copying a mansion that stood in Dublin, and the cornerstone was laid in 1792. Although President John Adams first occupied the building in November 1800, work wasn't completed until a few years later. In August 1814, the British burned the building, gutting the interior but leaving the stone shell. The exterior wall behind the portico is the only part of the north front that dates from the 1790s; the remainder of the stonework, being fire-damaged, was replaced when the building was rebuilt between 1815 and 1817. The south front survived the fire intact, and its portico was added in 1824. The north portico, visible here, dates from 1829. In

20 October 1995

1902 the interior, by then cramped and structurally unsound, was heavily remodeled by President Theodore Roosevelt, and two wings (not visible here) were added to the exterior. The famous oval office is in the west wing (outside the frame to the right in the recent photograph). First occupied by President Taft in 1909, the office was moved to its present location in a 1934 remodeling. During the Truman administration, the interior structure of the White House was found to be dangerously deteriorated; to repair it, the building's interior was completely gutted and rebuilt in concrete and steel. Today, few of the interior archtectural details predate these renovations. The statue of Jefferson was removed from the grounds in 1874, and today it resides in the Capitol.

Pennsylvania Avenue looking east from the Treasury Building. On a rainy day in March 1912, the unidentified remains of sixty-four victims of the battleship U.S.S. *Maine* were carried down Pennsylvania Avenue on their way to Arlington Cemetery. The *Maine* was destroyed by a mysterious explosion in Havana Harbor in 1898, leading to war with Spain, which was then occupying Cuba. Most of the 266 victims of the disaster were buried in Arlington Cemetery in 1899; these additional victims were found when the hulk was raised from the harbor bottom in 1912. Delivered by ship to the Navy Yard in southeast Washington, the remains were carried through the city to ceremonies at the State, War, and Navy Building (now the Old Executive Office Building). Afterwards, a parade escorted the caskets through Georgetown and across the Aqueduct Bridge to

21 April 1996

Arlington Cemetery. The building on the left with Doric columns is the Willard Hotel, built in 1901, replacing the original Willard building of 1850. In the center is the Old Post Office Building, with its prominent clock tower, completed in 1899. Just in front, surmounted by a mansard tower bearing a flag, is the Southern Railway Building, built in stages at the end of the nineteenth century and destroyed by fire in 1916. The block on the right was demolished around 1930 for construction of the Department of Commerce Building. Depression-era financial constraints limited the extent of the Commerce Building, however, and the site remained vacant until World War II, when a temporary building occupied the block. Today it is the site of Pershing Park.

c. 1900

Pennsylvania Avenue looking east from the Old Post Office Building. The unusual windmill-topped structure on the left was built in 1884 for Alderney Dairies. The windmill originally pumped water from a well in the basement to a holding tank in the roof. By the time of this photograph the building was occupied by a moving company, and the windmill had presumably fallen into disuse. The device disappeared within a few years, but the building survived until 1955. The two blocks in the foreground remained relatively intact until they were demolished in 1967 for the construction of the FBI Building. Widely criticized, the enormous fortress-like structure is unattractive and architecturally out of sync with its neighbors on Pennsylvania Avenue. Originally, shops were intended to fill the spaces between the pillars on the ground floor, but J. Edgar Hoover rejected the plan on security grounds and today the spaces are blocked by concrete panels.

14 March 1996

6 July 1955

Looking east on D Street and Pennsylvania Avenue from Eleventh Street. This photograph was taken on the sixth day of a transit strike in 1955. Ordinarily, commuters were not allowed to park on the streetcar tracks, as they have here. The building on the point of the triangular block, between Pennsylvania Avenue (right) and D Street (center), was originally a bank, but by 1955 it housed the Penn Restaurant. The block was demolished in 1967 for the construction of the FBI Building, visible in the center of the recent photograph. Two entire city blocks were razed and a one-block section of D Street was closed and filled by the new building. Over one hundred small businesses were forced to close or relocate.

21 September 1995

c. 1900

Ninth Street looking north from Pennsylvania Avenue. Many of the nineteenth-century commercial buildings in the photograph below survived until relatively recent times, outlasting the area's commercial prosperity by many years. The block on the left was razed in 1967 for the construction of the FBI Building.

The Academy of Music Building, with a square tower, was razed in 1952; the site was later occupied by a parking garage, itself since demolished. The building on the far right survived until 1984 when it was demolished for the Market Square project.

6 April 1996

May 1865

Market Square looking east from Pennsylvania Avenue and Ninth Street. Celebrating victory in the Civil War, the Grand Review of the Army of the Republic was perhaps the greatest parade in the city's history. For two days, some 200,000 officers and men marched down Pennsylvania Avenue and past a reviewing stand near the White House. Many of the flags hung in tatters, and the troops were dressed as they had been in battle, their uniforms faded and stained. It was quite a spectacle. In the photograph below, horse-drawn ambulances can be seen to the left, taking up the rear of a column of troops. In the center is the head of the next column, led by mounted officers. The *Evening Star* wrote about the seemingly endless procession:

12 September 1995

"More tattered flags, more rifles whose bullets had sung the death song of many a foe, and ambulances from whose shining cushions the flecks of blood wrung out in agony seemed not yet to have been wholly wiped away." Three federal-style houses, each with dormer windows, can be seen to the left in the early photograph, on either side of Eighth Street. Such houses, built in the early decades of the eighteenth century, once lined the entire length of Pennsylvania Avenue from the Capitol to Georgetown. Only a few remain today.

12 November 1970

Market Square looking northeast from Pennsylvania Avenue and Ninth Street. Pennsylvania Avenue has always been the city's most important thoroughfare, but by 1970 it was looking rather seedy. Since that time, the avenue has been rehabilitated by a combination of public and private forces led by the Pennsylvania Avenue Development Corporation (PADC), a federal agency. The PADC condemned land along the avenue and sold or leased it to cooperative developers. Market Square, which fills the recent view, was one such project. Constructed in the late 1980s, it houses shops, offices, and apartments. In the photograph below are four commercial buildings dating from the turn of the century. Between them, jarring and incongruous, is a bank built in 1962. On the right is Kann's Department Store. Kann's occupied a storefront here in the 1890s and expanded over the decades until it filled most of the block. The decline of retail business downtown forced the store to close in 1975. It was demolished in 1979 after being severely damaged by fire.

28 September 1995

c. 1903

Seventh Street looking north from Pennsylvania Avenue. The building on the right, at the corner of Seventh Street and Indiana Avenue, was built for the Firemen's Insurance Company in 1883. The present dome is a recent reconstruction—the original had disappeared by the 1930s. On the left is the Saks and Company building, built in 1884. Saks and Company, now Saks Fifth Avenue, was established on this site in 1867. In 1932 the building was acquired by Kann's Department Store for its own expanding operations. It was damaged by fire in 1979 and demolished shortly thereafter. Today, Market Square occupies the site.

6 April 1996

1917

Tenth Street looking south towards B Street (now Constitution Avenue) and the National Museum (now the National Museum of Natural History). At the time of the photograph below, much of the seventy-acre triangle between Constitution and Pennsylvania avenues was given over to light industry and trade. The western portion of the triangle held the city's red-light district, while the northern fringe, along Pennsylvania Avenue, was lined with restaurants, cheap hotels, and similar establishments. Historically, the low-lying area had been prone to flooding, consigning it to marginal uses. By the early twentieth century, the triangle was considered a blight on the capital, given its proximity to the Mall and Pennsylvania Avenue, Washington's ceremonial thoroughfare. By 1929 a project was under way to clear the area and replace the existing structures with monumental federal office buildings. The Internal Revenue Service Building, on the right in the recent view, was begun that year and completed in 1935. The Justice Department Building, on the left, was started somewhat later but finished in 1934. In the center of each view is the National Museum, now the National Museum of Natural History. It was completed in 1911.

22 March 1996

1927

The northeast corner of Tenth Street and Louisiana Avenue. The wedge of land between Pennsylvania Avenue, Constitution Avenue, and Fifteenth Street was changed so dramatically by the Federal Triangle project in the 1930s that today it is difficult to get one's bearings when regarding a photograph from the earlier era. Many streets that ran through the triangle were truncated or eliminated entirely as smaller blocks were cleared, consolidated, and filled with government office buildings. Louisiana Avenue, on the right in the photograph below, ran a block east to Center Market; at the time, this neighborhood was a busy wholesale and retail food market. This photograph was taken by Joseph Bishop in 1927, perhaps because an air of doom hung over the neighborhood. Within a few years, the block would be demolished for the construction of the Justice Department Building, which fills the recent view. Completed in 1934, the leviathan structure covers the area between Ninth and Tenth streets from Constitution Avenue to Pennsylvania Avenue.

27 August 1995

c. 1901

Looking west on C Street from Twelfth Street. Federal Triangle was once a notorious red-light district. During the Civil War, troops flocked to the area in search of saloons and brothels. Robberies and brawls were commonplace. Freed slaves lived in Murder Bay, a slum of tightly packed hovels between Thirteenth and Fifteenth streets. There, amid filth and squalor, all manner of crime and vice flourished. After the war, the brothels continued, albeit on a smaller scale. Well past the turn of the century, C Street, pictured below, and Ohio Avenue, a half-block from here, were notorious for their houses of ill-repute. In the 1930s the area was radically transformed by the Federal Triangle project. Six blocks of C Street were closed and filled with various government buildings, and Ohio Avenue was eliminated entirely. The building in the recent view is the new Post Office Building, built in 1934. The vantage point of the photograph is somewhat to the southwest of the Old Post Office Building. Twelfth Street, in the foreground, has been widened considerably.

14 August 1995

1929

B Street (now Constitution Avenue) and Seventh Street, looking northwest. Center Market was where Washingtonians shopped for fresh meat, fish, fruit, and vegetables in the days before supermarkets and refrigeration. This view shows the rear of the building—the front faced Pennsylvania Avenue with two imposing entrances, each with two towers. Inside were spaces for many hundreds of vendors. Indeed, at the time of its construction in 1871, it was the largest market building in the country. This site had been the location of the city's principal market since the first years of the nineteenth century. The Washington Canal ran along what is now Constitution Avenue, in the foreground, and boats carried produce directly to market. In 1872, the canal's waters were run through large culverts and B Street (later renamed Constitution Avenue) was laid on top. When the photograph below was taken in 1929, the Federal Triangle project was already under way. On the far left, the new Internal Revenue Service Building can be seen under construction. Two years later, Center Market was demolished for construction of the National Archives. The market building wasn't replaced— the proliferation of local food stores was changing the way Washingtonians shopped for food, and other markets around the city were able to take up the slack. Washington's other market houses were similar to, but smaller than, Center Market. Of these, only Eastern Market on Capitol Hill still fills its original function.

17 November 1995

c. 1888

C Street looking west from Third Street. In the mid-nineteenth century, the neighborhood around Judiciary Square was one of the finest and most fashionable in the city. By the 1870s, however, the area began to fall into disfavor as newer neighborhoods to the northwest, centered along Connecticut Avenue, opened to development. In the 1930s many of the fine houses in the area were demolished for various government buildings. The large structure in the center of the recent view is the District Municipal Building, built in 1940. The house in the photograph below was probably built around 1875. It was razed in 1939.

29 August 1995

c. 1901

G Street looking west from Fifth Street. This photograph was taken on the eastern fringe of Washington's downtown, looking west towards the heart of the old business district. Downtown is bordered by Pennsylvania Avenue on the south, Fifteenth Street and the White House on the west, Fifth Street and the environs of Judiciary Square on the east, and New York Avenue and K Street on the north. Obscuring the view westward in the recent view is the MCI Center arena, home to the Washington Wizards basketball team and the Washington Capitals hockey team. Completed in 1997, the arena spans one and a half city blocks and necessitated the closure of G Street between Sixth and Seventh streets. The fine Second Empire–style building on the right, probably constructed around 1875, now houses a Burger King restaurant.

18 January 1998

c. 1917

F Street looking west from Sixth Street. The MCI Center arena, on the right in the recent view, opened in 1997. In spite of its vast bulk, the structure harmonizes nicely with the historic buildings on adjacent streets, and in deference to city height limits, half of the 20,000 seats are below street level. The photograph below was taken around 1917, when F Street was the center of commercial activity in the city. Most of the buildings in the photograph were still standing in the early 1970s when they were acquired by a city agency intent on redeveloping the block. The assembled parcel was offered to developers in 1973, but plans repeatedly fell through. The last tenant left in 1980 and the remaining buildings were demolished in 1985. The site remained vacant until 1995, when work on the arena was begun.

19 December 1997

c. 1908

The northwest corner of Seventh and G streets. The building on the corner was constructed around 1865 and has served many uses since. At the time of this photograph, the Merchants and Mechanics Savings Bank had recently expanded into the structure from smaller quarters at 707 G Street. Later, during World War I, a drug store occupied the storefront, followed by a phonograph shop, then two dress shops. The last tenant was Kent Jewelers, which left in the early 1990s. The two men in the photograph below are cleaning the conduits beneath the streetcar tracks. The conduits held rails that supplied the cars with electricity.

12 August 1995

c. 1901

Seventh Street looking north towards G Street. Careful inspection of the photograph below will reveal a group of three federal-style buildings directly in the center of the view, each three stories tall. Before the Civil War, such buildings lined the streets downtown, but today only a few remain. The bottom floors held shops, while the upper floors were generally home to the shopkeepers and their families. Seventh Street and Pennsylvania Avenue were the principal commercial streets in those days and the surrounding blocks were largely residential. Later in the nineteenth century, as the city grew, commerce spread to F and G streets. Most of the buildings in this view date from that period, when commercial buildings, many four stories tall and topped with elaborate wooden cornices, replaced the smaller federal structures. Seventh Street's prosperity lasted through World War II, but it died in the 1950s and 1960s and has never fully recovered. The MCI Center arena, on the right in the recent view, was completed in 1997. It is expected to bring new life to Seventh Street and the surrounding blocks.

19 December 1997

c. 1901

H Street looking east from Seventh Street. Today, the intersection of Seventh and H streets is the center of Washington's Chinatown, but at the turn of the century, it had a German flavor. Seventh Street was a bustling commercial corridor, and many Germans, both Catholics and Jews, lived and owned shops in the surrounding blocks. At the time Chinatown was located on Pennsylvania Avenue near Fourth Street, N.W. Around 1930 federal construction projects obliterated that neighborhood and many Chinese businesses relocated to the block on H Street between Sixth and Seventh streets. Washington's Chinatown was never very large, and today about 500 Chinese Americans live in the neighborhood. Only a fraction of the property is Chinese owned; about ten shops and two dozen restaurants make up the Chinese district. Certainly the most striking symbol of the Chinese presence is the arch spanning H Street, visible in the recent view. Built in 1986, it was a collaborative effort between Washington and its sister-city, Beijing.

12 August 1995

c. 1915

The southeast corner of Ninth and E streets. At one time Ninth Street was the center of Washington's theater district. On the corner in the photograph below is the Joy Theatre, which opened in 1914. Summertime audiences no doubt appreciated its "Typhoon Cooling System," a primitive form of air conditioning in which fans blew air over large blocks of ice. The Joy Theatre closed around 1924 and the building was remodeled to house a store. On the right is Moore's Garden Theatre, which operated for many years under several names, most recently as the Gayety. The majority of the block was eventually acquired by the Pennsylvania Avenue Development Corporation, a federal agency. Development of the parcel was delayed, however, when Washington's real estate market collapsed in 1990. In 1996 work began on Market Square North, a project that will include shops, offices, and apartments.

11 March 1998

c. 1901

F Street looking east from Ninth Street. The distinctive Le Droit building, in the center of the photograph below, was built in 1875. On the far right is the Warder Building, built in 1892 and later renamed the Atlas. Shops lined the first floor, while the upper floors held offices, many occupied by patent attorneys attracted by the proximity of the Patent Office, across the street. By the 1950s the aging building was half vacant, and a decade later it was almost empty. Adult book stores occupied some of the storefronts in the 1980s and 1990s. The last such establishment departed in 1996, and today the building is vacant. On the far left surrounded by an iron fence are the monumental steps of the Patent Building, removed in 1936 to improve traffic flow on F Street. In the 1970s the city turned this block of F Street into a pedestrian mall in an unsuccessful attempt to spruce up the blighted area. The mall only hurt business though—it impeded access to the stores and became a gathering place for vagrants. In 1997 the mall was removed and the street reopened to traffic.

16 February 1998

c. 1900

F Street looking west from Ninth Street. At the time of this photograph, F Street was one of the principal shopping streets in the city. In the foreground is the fence of the Patent Office; in the distance, at the opposite end of F Street, is the colonnade of the Treasury Building, on Fifteenth Street. In between is an array of commercial buildings, the vast majority built in the late nineteenth century. On the right in both views is the Old Masonic Hall, designed in the style of the Italian Renaissance. Its cornerstone was laid in 1868 in a ceremony attended by President Andrew Johnson, himself a Mason. Shops occupied the ground floor, while the second floor held a large hall used for society functions. On the third and fourth floors were the masonic lodge rooms. The Julius Lansburgh Furniture Company moved into the building in 1921 and did business there until the 1970s. Since then, it has remained vacant.

12 January 1998

c. 1920

Ninth Street looking south from G Street. Construction of the impressive classical revival structure on the left was begun in 1836 and continued in stages for thirty-one years. From 1840 to 1932 it housed the Patent Office, and other agencies used it as well. During this period a museum occupied part of the building; the principal attraction was a collection of patent models of important American inventions. Today it is home to two Smithsonian museums: the National Portrait Gallery and the National Museum of American Art. During the Civil War, the structure served as a hospital, which Walt Whitman often visited, providing care and comfort to the wounded soldiers. After the Patent Office moved out in 1932, the building was occupied for three decades by the Civil Service Commission. In the 1950s the General Services Administration planned to demolish the landmark for a parking lot, but fortunately, it was instead transferred to the Smithsonian Institution. The building on the right in the recent photograph has been home to the YWCA since 1981.

11 January 1996

1900

Ford's Theater, looking northeast across Tenth Street. The site of one of the nation's greatest tragedies, Ford's Theater has been restored and opened to the public with a working theater and a museum documenting the life and death of Abraham Lincoln. Built in 1863 by John T. Ford, the building had served as a theater for only two years when President Lincoln was assassinated there on the night of April 14, 1865. He had come to see the comedy "Our American Cousin," destined to be the last performance at the theater for more than a hundred years. After the assassination, Ford's plans to reopen the theater were thwarted and the building was acquired by the federal government. It was remodeled and used for offices, and for a time, the Army Medical Museum was housed here. In 1893 a partial collapse of the building killed twenty-two government workers; after that time, it was used only for storage. A museum of Lincoln artifacts opened here in 1932, and in the 1960s, the building was restored to its appearance as of the night of Lincoln's death. Theater performances resumed in 1968.

7 August 1995

December 1911

F Street looking west from Tenth Street. The Woodward and Lothrop department store, a venerable Washington institution for over one hundred years, closed its doors for the last time in November 1995. In 1880, S. Walter Woodward and Alvin M. Lothrop opened their first Washington dry goods store at 705 Market Space (now Pennsylvania Avenue), several blocks from here. In 1887 they moved to the Carlisle Building (in the center of the photograph below, at the left end of the block), on the corner of F and Eleventh streets. By 1911 Woodies had expanded to fill the entire block on F Street, except for Rich's

shoe store on the far right. Shortly thereafter the four old buildings between the Carlisle and Rich's were demolished and replaced with the present eight-story structure. The building achieved its final form in 1926 after the demolition of the Carlisle. In 1994 Woodies went bankrupt, largely the victim of competition from more fashionable department stores. Woodward and Lothrop, by this time a chain of many stores, was sold, but no one wanted the enormous downtown flagship store. In 1996 the building was bought by the Washington Opera for conversion to an opera house.

9 August 1995

15 October 1928

Looking west on E Street from Eleventh Street. The appearance of the *Graf Zeppelin* over the capital on this gray October day was a great surprise, and Washingtonians filled the streets as horns and whistles blew in greetings to the great airship. Almost the length of an ocean liner (775 feet) and capable of eighty miles an hour, the *Graf Zeppelin* was a truly spectacular sight. Launched for the first time in September 1928, only a month earlier, the airship was on the final leg of an exhibition flight from Friedrichshafen, Germany, to Lakehurst, New Jersey. It was the first transoceanic flight by airship with paying passengers, and at 6,200 miles, the longest nonstop flight ever made up to that time. The airborne leviathan had followed a southerly route across the Atlantic, to avoid bad weather, and was to have followed the coast northward to Lakehurst, but a

29 June 1996

last-minute change in itinerary brought it over Washington instead. Arriving from the east, it passed the Capitol, flew over northeast Washington, then turned and headed for the White House. President Coolidge, warned of its imminent arrival, hurried outside and watched as the airship circled the White House and then headed north to Baltimore and Philadelphia on its way to Lakehurst. Later, in the 1930s, the *Graf Zeppelin* flew regular passenger flights from Germany to Brazil, a route popular with the large German colony there, and never suffered an accident. It was retired from passenger service immediately after the airship *Hindenburg* exploded, in 1937, and was scrapped in 1940.

1922

The southeast corner of Eleventh and F streets. When the photograph below was taken in 1922, F Street was at its height as a shopping district. After World War II the area declined, and by the 1980s the fur shops and haberdashers had been replaced by wig shops and liquor stores. In the late 1980s the lots on this block were bought up by a developer and assembled into a large parcel, but the real estate market crashed in 1990, and an office building planned for the site was never built.

12 August 1995

10 September 1966

The east side of Eleventh Street between E and F streets.
When the photograph below was taken in 1966, Downtown
still appeared quite lively and prosperous. In fact, business had
dropped off considerably since 1950, when suburban shopping
malls began to siphon shoppers away from Downtown. The
coup de grâce came in 1968, with the riots following the assassination of Martin Luther King, Jr. Downtown had not been
heavily damaged in the disturbances, but suburban shoppers no
longer felt comfortable there, and business took a dramatic turn
for the worse. Throughout the 1960s and 1970s civic and
business leaders tried to reverse the trend, but with little success.
The 1980s saw a building boom in Washington, and many of
the small lots downtown were assembled by developers into
larger parcels suitable for office buildings. A large project including office space and a multiscreen theater was planned for
this site in the late 1980s but was abandoned when Washington's real estate market crashed in 1990.

30 June 1995

1923

The east side of Eleventh Street between E and F streets. In the photograph below, a horse and carriage can be seen parked along the curb among the early automobiles, the animal no doubt oblivious to the march of progress. By the 1920s, when this photograph was taken, horses had largely been supplanted as a means of transportation, but they were still a common sight in downtown Washington. The ascendancy of the automobile had at least one positive effect on the city: when the livery stables that once lined the alleyways were converted to automobile garages, the ubiquitous flies that plagued Downtown disap-

30 June 1995

peared. On the left is another sight considered an anacronism
today: a baby has been left unattended in front of a shop while
its mother shops inside.

1920

The southeast corner of Twelfth and H streets. During the 1950s and 1960s, new construction in downtown Washington fell off rapidly as the area deteriorated. Instead, most new construction occurred to the west, in Midtown, in the area centered around Connecticut Avenue and K Street. By the 1970s the vicinity of Twelfth and H streets was a wasteland of vacant lots and deteriorating buildings. During the building boom of the 1980s, however, the large office blocks that filled Midtown spread eastward into this portion of the old downtown, and today the area is filled with a seamless array of office buildings and hotels.

13 August 1995

1920

G Street, looking east towards Twelfth Street. Before World War II, Downtown accounted for the vast majority of retail sales in the metropolitan area, and goods and services of every conceivable sort were available here. After the war, the city grew dramatically, but sales in the city center declined as shoppers turned to the suburbs. Downtown hit bottom in the 1970s, when dozens of adult book stores and theaters studded the area but little else could survive among the vacant lots and derelict buildings. Since that time, conditions have improved considerably. The construction of the Metrorail system in the 1970s and the convention center in the 1980s helped bring people back to the area. Many new office buildings were

constructed in the '80s as development spread eastward from Midtown. Finally, the development of Pennsylvania Avenue by the Pennsylvania Avenue Development Corporation, a federal agency, had a salutary effect on the blocks north of the Avenue. Today, Downtown is lively during the day but deserted after dark, when office workers have returned home to the suburbs.

In contrast to many other cities, very few people live in downtown Washington. Encouraging the construction of apartments here has long been an important goal of city planners, but developers have little financial incentive, since office space is so much more profitable.

c. 1901

G Street looking west from Thirteenth Street. When the cornerstone of Epiphany Church was laid in 1843, this block of G Street was a residential area and parishioners walked to services. President James Buchanan attended church here, as did Jefferson Davis and many other well-known Washingtonians. In 1857 the structure was remodeled, doubling in size, and a tower, visible in the photograph below, was added. During the Civil War, the church served for a time as a hospital for wounded troops. When the neighborhood became commercialized at the end of the nineteenth century, Epiphany remained when many other congregations left the area, and today the structure is a fine counterpoint to the boxy office buildings that line G Street. The present tower dates from a remodeling in 1922.

12 August 1995

c. 1920

Looking west on New York Avenue and H Street from Thirteenth Street. The photograph below was taken from the old Masonic Temple on Thirteenth Street, today the National Museum of Women in the Arts. To the left is New York Avenue, heading towards the White House, three blocks away; to the right is H Street. In the center, occupying the triangular lot, is the New York Avenue Presbyterian Church, frequented by

President Lincoln during the Civil War. The steeple, lost in a storm in 1898, wasn't replaced until 1929. The church was demolished in 1950 by its congregation and replaced by a new sanctuary, twice as large but lacking the charm and historical connections of the older structure. On the left in the recent photograph is the enormous Daon Building, completed in 1983 and now home to the Inter-American Development Bank.

27 October 1995

1915

G Street looking east from the north yard of the Treasury Building. Fifteenth Street, in the vicinity of the Treasury, was the city's financial district and a prestigious address for lawyers and bankers. Today, the surviving Beaux-Arts facades form an appropriately grand setting for the Treasury Building and the inaugural parades that pass this spot every four years. The Riggs Building, on the right, was completed in 1912. It was home to the Keith Theater, which opened in 1913 as a vaudeville theater and later showed films. It closed in 1978. In 1986, the building's facade was incorporated into Metropolitan Square, an office and retail complex that now fills most of the block. On the left in the photograph below is the Home Life Building, built in 1901. It was replaced by the Washington Building, completed in 1927 and remodeled in 1986.

30 January 1996

5 March 1913

Fourteenth Street looking north from L Street towards Thomas Circle. The Portland, on the left in the photograph below, surmounted by a short spire, was built in 1880 as the city's first luxury apartment building. At the time of the photograph, Thomas Circle was a genteel neighborhood of apartment houses and large homes. A number of shops were located on this block, including grocery stores, cleaners, tailors, barbers, and the like. On the upper floors were apartments. In later years the park around the circle was carved up to accommodate increased traffic, while many of the older structures were replaced by bland office buildings, hotels, and apartment blocks that dwarfed the circle in scale. The Portland was demolished in 1962 and replaced with the present office building four years later. The only structure in common between the two photographs, other than the statue of General George H. Thomas in the center of the circle, is the neo-Gothic Luther Place Memorial Church, built in 1870.

13 August 1995

c. 1880

K Street looking east towards Fourteenth Street. Today "K Street architecture" is a pejorative term denoting glass-box office buildings, each built to the maximum size allowable by law. In the late nineteenth century however, K Street was perhaps the finest residential street in the city. These elaborate rowhouses were built around 1875, when the neighborhood was new and fashionable. Around 1920, K Street between Ninth and Sixteenth streets began to fill with office buildings, and by the 1930s the process was complete. These rowhouses were razed and replaced with two small office buildings, a gas station, and other unnoteworthy structures, themselves since demolished. The three buildings on the left in the recent photograph were built in the 1950s and 1960s. At the end of the same block stands the Tower Building, built in 1929 and remodeled in 1997.

17 April 1996

c. 1937

K Street looking east from Farragut Square. Most of the residential structures on this block of K Street survived until after World War II, although by the 1930s many served as offices for real estate agents, construction firms, architects, and the like, while restaurants occupied the ground floor in many of the old houses. On the left in the photograph below is the third house of Shepherd's Row, a reminder of K Street's heyday as a fashionable residential district, and at the time of this photograph, home to the Washington Club. In the center is the Young Women's Christian Association Building, dedicated in 1927. The building was sold in 1978 after the association decided it could not be renovated at reasonable cost, and it was demolished three years later and replaced by the present office building.

17 August 1995

c. 1887

Seventeenth Street looking north from I Street. While today Farragut Square is at the heart of the city's new business district, at one time it was a fashionable residential neighborhood, home to many of the city's most prominent citizens. The statue of Admiral Farragut forms a common reference point in the center of the square; beyond it, leading northwest, is Connecticut Avenue; to the right, stretching towards the horizon, is Seventeenth Street. In the center of the earlier view is Shepherd's Row, built in 1872 on what was then the northern fringe of the city. The leftmost house was first occupied by Alexander Shepherd, governor of the District of Columbia. Later, in the 1920s, it was converted to a restaurant and offices. After World War II a building boom began in Midtown; Shepherd's Row was demolished in 1952 and replaced by the present office building. The statue of Admiral Farragut, dedicated in 1881, was the work of Vinnie Ream Hoxie, a prominent woman sculptor. Farragut is best known for his naval assault on Mobile Bay in 1864, in which he cried, "Damn the torpedoes! Full speed ahead!" The statue itself was cast from the propeller of the U.S.S. *Hartford,* the admiral's flagship during that famous engagement.

1 February 1997

15 October 1951

Eighteenth Street looking north from L Street. Washington's Midtown lies, roughly speaking, between the White House and Dupont Circle, west of Fifteenth Street and the old downtown, and east of New Hampshire Avenue. Originally a residential neighborhood, Midtown was gradually converted to commercial use, beginning around 1920. After World War II the process escalated dramatically as many new office buildings were constructed in the area. In the center of the photograph below is the Ring Building, a twelve-story office building built in 1946. The buildings on the left in the recent photo were constructed in the 1980s and 1990s.

19 August 1995

October 1949

The southeast corner of Twentieth and K streets. When the photograph below was taken, commercial development had not yet spread this far west on K Street, and the area was dominated by apartment buildings. The gas station on the corner was built in 1924 and demolished in 1966. The present office building was constructed in 1977.

20 April 1996

January 1913

Looking northwest across Connecticut Avenue towards Jefferson Street. The three commercial buildings in the photograph below were constructed around 1910, replacing brick rowhouses built thirty years earlier. The one on the far left was demolished in 1931 and replaced the same year with the present Moorish Revival structure.

27 August 1995

c. 1890

Connecticut Avenue looking north from N Street towards Dupont Circle. The Connecticut Avenue of 1890 would seem a very alien place to today's Washingtonian, with its quiet streets and elaborate Victorian mansions. On the left is the British Legation, built in 1872 on what was then a frontier of the city. At that time the neighborhood had recently been opened to development by the civic improvements of Alexander Shepherd, first as vice-president of the Board of Public Works, then as governor of the District of Columbia. In the early 1870s, Shepherd transformed the city by paving streets, laying sidewalks, installing sewers and gas lights, and planting trees at a frenetic pace and fantastic cost. Shepherd left the city bankrupt but transformed into a modern, world-class city. Just to right of the British Legation is Phillips Row, seven elegant houses constructed in 1878. In the distance, on Dupont Circle, is Stewart's Castle, built in 1873 by mining magnate and U.S. senator William Stewart. By 1890 the house was serving as the Chinese Legation; it was razed in 1901. Later, commercial development spread into this block, and by the 1950s the British Legation had been replaced by a gas station, while Philips Row had become a parking lot. Today the block is solidly occupied by office buildings.

5 March 1996

c. 1890

Looking north on Connecticut Avenue from R Street. This fine mansion was built in 1888 by Philetus Sawyer, a United States senator. It was demolished in 1923 and replaced by the present commercial building, now home to La Tomate Restaurant.

25 August 1995

The northwest corner of Columbia Road and Wyoming Avenue. Managasset, the home of George Truesdell, once occupied a four-acre lot bounded by Columbia Road, Kalorama Road, and Nineteenth Street. Truesdell, a real estate developer, built the house around 1890 and later demolished it for the construction of the Altamont, a luxury apartment building. Opened in 1916, the Altamont had two huge twelve-room apartments on each of the three upper floors. These apartments each had four bedrooms and three baths, plus two bedrooms and a bath for servants. Truesdell later sold the building, and the large apartments were broken up into smaller units. Originally a rental building, the Altamont was converted to a cooperative in 1949.

30 October 1995

1934

Looking east at the intersection of Columbia Road and Eighteenth Street from the Melwood Apartments. Today's Adams Morgan was laid out at the end of the nineteenth century as several suburban subdivisions, including Washington Heights, Lanier Heights, and others. The appellation Adams Morgan dates only from the 1950s, derived from the names of two public schools that served the area. Before World War II Adams Morgan was an upscale residential neighborhood, but during the war the area began to decline, as many of the large, single-family homes were broken up into apartments and rooming houses. In the 1950s many whites left for the suburbs, after desegregation of the public schools. Large-scale redevelopment of the area was considered in the 1960s, but fortunately never implemented, and since the 1980s Adams Morgan has enjoyed a renaissance. In the photograph below, the streetcar on the right is heading towards Chevy Chase. The tracks led from Eighteenth Street to Calvert Street, across Rock Creek Park, and then right onto Connecticut Avenue. The tracks on Columbia Road terminated at Mount Pleasant.

18 July 1997

1 April 1951

Looking south at the intersection of Columbia Road and Eighteenth Street. The Knickerbocker Theater (later the Ambassador), in the center of the photograph below, was the scene of the worst disaster in Washington's history. During a showing on Saturday, January 28, 1922, the roof of the theater collapsed, killing ninety-eight persons and injuring more than a hundred. The immediate cause was a tremendous load of snow on the roof: twenty-six inches had fallen in the previous day, one of the heaviest snowfalls in the city's history. Later it was learned that the ceiling beams extended only two inches into the supporting walls, the result of shoddy construction work. Although he was not at fault, the building's architect was ruined by the disaster and later committed suicide. Originally constructed in 1917, the Knickerbocker was rebuilt after the tragedy and reopened in 1923 as the Ambassador. It remained in operation until 1969, when the building was demolished. The site remained vacant for a decade and is now occupied by a branch of Crestar Bank. The building on the left was built as a private residence around 1900. Shortly thereafter it was converted to commercial use and housed a People's Drug Store for many years. Today it is home to a McDonald's restaurant.

20 October 1995

1908

Woodley Park and Rock Creek Valley looking northwest from the Mendota Apartments. As late as 1908, Woodley Park still had a distinctly rural appearance. Although the area had been subdivided on paper, few of the lots had been developed. These photographs were taken from the Mendota, at Kalorama Road and Twentieth Street in Kalorama Triangle. Built in 1901, the Mendota is one of the oldest apartment buildings in the city.

On the right in the earlier view is the old Rock Creek Bridge, built in 1891 to carry trolley tracks across Rock Creek Valley. It was replaced by the Calvert Street Bridge (later renamed the Duke Ellington Bridge), completed in 1935. On the left in both views is the Taft Bridge, built between 1897 and 1907. Carrying Connecticut Avenue across the valley, the Taft Bridge helped open Northwest Washington to residential development.

11 April 1996

1903

Looking west across Connecticut Avenue towards Newark Street. In the late nineteenth century, the area that became Cleveland Park was still rural. A number of large country estates were located here, including that of President Grover Cleveland. In the 1890s some new subdivisions, including Cleveland Park, were carved out of the old estates. The photograph below was taken from an advertisement published by a real estate firm in 1903. Cleveland Park had about fifty houses at that time, most of which have survived. The houses were large, and every one was different, many designed by prominent architects. The stone building on the left, built by the developer, was a community center and served as shelter for the trolley stop. The houses on the right are still standing today but are obscured in the recent photograph by trees and several houses of more recent vintage.

20 June 1996

c. 1923

The northeast corner of Fourteenth Street and Park Road. The Tivoli, the grandest of Washington's neighborhood theaters, opened in April 1924. This photograph shows workers placing finishing touches on the theater's exterior, an eclectic design influenced by Spanish Colonial architecture. The interior was equally imposing, with marble floors, crystal chandeliers, and exit signs made of leaded glass. The Tivoli initially showed silent films, and in 1928 became the first neighborhood theater to install a sound system. At the time, Columbia Heights was an upscale residential neighborhood, but in later years it declined dramatically. In 1968 the commercial strip along Fourteenth Street was devastated in the riots following the assassination of Martin Luther King, Jr. The Tivoli survived, only to close in 1976. Since that time, vandalism and the elements have taken their toll on the theater, as preservation groups, developers, and the city have fought over its fate. In 1985 the Tivoli was placed on the National Register of Historic Places, but its future remains uncertain.

30 October 1995

4 October 1949

U Street looking east from Thirteenth Street. From the 1920s through the 1940s, U Street was Washington's "Black Broadway." At the time, downtown theaters, clubs, and restaurants were off limits to black Washingtonians. Instead, they came to U Street for entertainment, and the night life was dazzling. All of the top black entertainers played here, and some, like Duke Ellington, grew up in the neighborhood. The Lincoln Theatre, built in 1921, featured both stage acts and first-run movies. The theater was owned by whites, but the management was overwhelmingly black, as were the audiences. The exterior of the theater was relatively plain, but the interior was opulent, decorated with marble, chandeliers, and elaborate plaster work. Indeed, it was one of the finest theaters for black audiences in the country. While U Street enjoyed its heyday through the 1940s, it declined rapidly in the '50s as desegregation cost black businesses their captive clientele. The Lincoln Theatre survived until 1982, showing grade-B and second-run films, as U Street was overrun by drugs and crime. Recently however, the area has begun to enjoy something of a renaissance. The Lincoln was reopened in 1994 after an extensive restoration.

20 September 1995

The northeast corner of Seventh and P streets. The commercial strip along Seventh Street north of M Street was devastated in the riots following the assassination of Martin Luther King, Jr. This smoldering shell on the corner of P Street once housed New Deal Liquors and a rooming house. Overall, 900 businesses in the city were damaged during the riots, and twelve persons killed. Besides Seventh Street, the areas hardest hit were Fourteenth Street north of U Street and the commercial strip along H Street, N.E. The riots began on Thursday evening, April 4, following the news of King's assassination. The rioting that night was largely confined to Fourteenth Street and was controlled, with some difficulty, by District police.

Rioting broke out again on Friday and hit its peak that afternoon. Columns of smoke rose above the city as hundreds of stores were looted and burned. Much of the city was locked in a traffic jam as thousands of panicked commuters tried to leave the city early. District police escorted firemen as they frantically rushed from building to building, but, vastly outnumbered, the police were powerless to stop the rioting. Order was finally restored as 6,600 federal troops poured into the city Friday evening. Seventh Street itself has never recovered, and this lot at the corner of P Street is still vacant. Many of the other commercial buildings along Seventh Street that were destroyed in the riots have since been replaced with public housing.

6 November 1995

Barry Place looking west from Georgia Avenue. These modest shops once stood along Georgia Avenue opposite Howard University. They have long since disappeared, replaced by a McDonald's restaurant and a baseball field.

23 August 1995

7 March 1936

Fourth Street, N.E., looking south from the 2300 block towards Rhode Island Avenue. These boys waiting in front of the grocery store were no doubt hoping to earn some money carting groceries home in their wagons. The store itself was a member of the Sanitary Grocery chain, which had hundreds of locations in the Washington area. Formed in 1909, the chain was bought by Safeway Stores in 1928. The Sanitary name was used until 1941.

19 September 1995

29 March 1926

Michigan Avenue, N.E., looking southwest from Tenth Street. This short stretch of road was once part of Michigan Avenue, a major thoroughfare in Northeast Washington. Today, renamed Bunkerhill Road, it dead-ends at the Brookland Metro station, visible in the center of the recent photograph. Michigan Avenue now crosses the tracks on an overpass, to the right in the recent view. The Metrorail tracks follow the course of the Baltimore and Ohio Railroad's Metropolitan Branch, laid through here in 1873 and still in use. Beyond the tracks, to the west, is Catholic University, founded in 1887. The spire and dome of the adjacent National Shrine of the Immaculate Conception can be seen just above the overpass. To the east of the tracks is the Brookland neighborhood, laid out as a subdivision in 1887 on the farm of Colonel Jehiel Brooks. A largely white neighborhood until after World War II, Brookland is now mostly black. The large building on the left in the photograph below is DeSales Hall, home for many years to several Catholic religious communities.

2 February 1997

12 August 1950

Twenty-sixth Street looking north from Water Street. This photograph shows only a fraction of the fortresslike Heurich Brewery, which covered an entire city block. Inside were brewed Senate Beer, Old Georgetown Ale, Heurich's Lager, and many other varieties of beer. During Prohibition the building was idle, except for the ice plant, which remained in service until 1940. Beer was brewed here until 1956, when competition from large national breweries forced the plant to close. In 1961 the federal government condemned the building, to allow construction of approach ramps for the new Theodore Roosevelt Bridge. For a few years, the Arena Stage, a theater company, occupied the gymnasium in the old brewery. Today this one-time industrial neighborhood has been replaced with a maze of highways. In the recent photograph, the Watergate complex can be seen through the trees on the left.

23 August 1995

1941

The south side of Independence Avenue, S.W., between Sixth and Seventh streets. The photograph below shows work on a new streetcar line along Independence Avenue between Seventh (in the foreground) and First streets, S.W. Opened in 1941, the new line served the many federal buildings south of the Capitol.

Shortly after the photograph was taken, the houses in the background were demolished to allow the widening of Independence Avenue. Today the site is occupied by Federal Building 10B, which houses offices of the Department of Education.

29 June 1996

1949

Fourth Street, S.W., looking south between G and H streets. In 1949, when the photograph below was taken, Fourth Street was the principal commercial street in Southwest Washington. A close, vibrant community, Southwest was nevertheless considered one of the worst slums in the city. Much of the housing was appallingly bad: thousands of families lived by the light of kerosene lanterns and drew water from backyard spigots. In the mid-1950s, 550 acres of Southwest were razed in an urban renewal project, one of the first and most comprehensive in the nation. The shops in the photograph, and thousands of other buildings, were demolished, and over 10,000 persons were displaced. Built in their place were townhouses and high-rise apartments, a model community that was expected to draw middle-class families back into the city. Today, the new Southwest is neat but soulless, with a transient population of childless professionals rather than the stable, family-oriented community imagined by planners in the 1950s. In the recent photograph is the Capitol Park Apartments. Built around 1960, it was the first project in the redevelopment area to be completed.

6 December 1995

c. 1901

Four and one-half Street (now Fourth Street), S.W., looking south from I Street. Fourth Street was the main commercial street in the old Southwest and the dividing line between the races. Blacks lived to the east of Fourth Street (to the left in this view), while whites lived to the west. It was also the center of a large Jewish community. Al Jolson, vaudevillian and star of the first talking movie, *The Jazz Singer,* grew up here. His father, a rabbi, officiated at a nearby temple. Today, Jolson would find nothing recognizable. The lively commercial strip along Fourth Street was demolished in the late 1950s during urban renewal and replaced with Waterside Mall. The mall, on the left in the recent photograph, spans what was once Fourth Street.

26 February 1996

c. 1951

The northwest corner of Second and F streets, S.W. These houses on F Street were demolished in the mid-1950s as part of an urban renewal project that encompassed 550 acres and the destruction of thousands of buildings. This block was part of an eighty-acre pilot project, chosen for its proximity to the Capitol, only a few blocks away. More than half of the one thousand families that lived here had no electricity, indoor plumbing, or central heat. After the neighborhood was leveled, the Southwest Freeway (in the recent view) was built through here with little community opposition. Today the freeway separates the government office buildings to the north and the new residential area to the south. It also forms a barrier that divides and isolates the neighborhood.

13 December 1995

c. 1901

Looking east from the southwest corner of Second and E streets, S.W. Thousands of buildings were demolished in Southwest during the 1950s, and many of the streets were closed as well. One wonders what happened to Sullivan and his saloon; today the site is occupied by a parking lot and the neighborhood to the east has been replaced with a maze of highways. In the foreground of the recent photograph is the roof of a seafood restaurant, built in the middle of what was once Second Street. Beyond it is Interstate 395; to the right is an elevated span of the Southwest Freeway. The only building in the earlier photograph still standing is Dent School (on the horizon, with two chimneys) at Second and F streets, S.E. Today it houses the private Capitol Hill Day School.

18 October 1995

c. 1901

Looking northwest from the intersection of Delaware Avenue and E Street, S.W. On the corner is a carriage factory, demolished around 1907, along with its neighbors, for construction of the rail line. In the recent view, an Amtrak passenger train bound for Union Station is crossing a trestle over Interstate 395. E Street once ran westward from this point for many blocks, but today it dead-ends here, severed by the expressway.

16 April 1996

c. 1949

The south side of Pennsylvania Avenue, S.E., at the corner of Minnesota Avenue. Although many Washington neighborhoods have changed in racial composition over the years, the change in Anacostia was perhaps faster and more complete than anywhere else. When this photograph was taken around 1950, Anacostia's population was 82 percent white. Anacostia High School, the only high school in this part of the city, was strictly reserved for whites, while black students had to travel to schools in Northwest Washington. In 1954, when the city's schools were integrated, white families began to leave Anacostia, many relocating to nearby Prince Georges County. At the same time, the population of the metropolitan area was growing dramatically. With the lifting of restrictive housing covenants, blacks expanded into previously white in-town neighborhoods, while white population growth was concentrated in the suburbs. By 1960 the share of whites in Anacostia's population had fallen to 68 percent, and by 1970 it had dropped to 14 percent. In 1980, Anacostia was over 98 percent black.

22 March 1996

1916

The southeast corner of Nichols Avenue and Jefferson Street (now Martin Luther King Jr. Avenue and W Street), S.E. Uniontown, renamed Anacostia in 1886, was Washington's first suburban subdivision. It was laid out in 1854 on the east side of the Anacostia River, at the foot of the Eleventh Street Bridge, and became home to many workers at the Naval Yard across the river. While the original subdivision was only fifteen blocks in size, Anacostia now generally refers to the entire area east of the river and south of Pennsylvania Avenue, S.E. The photograph below was taken in 1916, probably on the occasion of a Fourth of July parade. The corner building in this Rockwellesque tableau was occupied by Bury's Drug Store. Today it is home to an office of the Social Services Division of the D.C. Superior Court.

31 October 1995

c. 1910

Nichols Avenue (now Martin Luther King Jr. Avenue), S.E., looking northeast from Howard Road. While Uniontown to the north was largely reserved for whites, Barry's Farm to the south has always been a black community. Founded shortly after the Civil War, Barry's Farm was a subdivision sponsored by the Freedmen's Bureau, a government agency. Freed slaves could purchase a building lot and enough wood for a small house, and pay by installment. By the turn of the century, Barry's Farm was a thriving community. On the left in both photographs is the old Birney School. Built in 1901 as an elementary school for black children, it is still standing but no longer in use. The trolley tracks were laid in the 1890s to serve Congress Heights, a newer development farther to the south. In those days Barry's Farm and the other communities east of the Anacostia River were like small towns, surrounded by countryside. It wasn't until World War II that the land between them began to be developed.

16 March 1997

c. 1865

Looking northwest towards Georgetown from Analostan (now Roosevelt) Island. A small settlement developed on the site of Georgetown in the 1740s, including a tobacco warehouse, a ferry landing, and a tavern. The city streets were first laid out in 1751, predating Washington by forty years. Through the end of the eighteenth century, Georgetown was a tobacco port, where merchants bought the weed from Maryland planters and loaded it onto ocean-going vessels for shipment overseas. By the time Washington was established in 1790, Georgetown was a bustling city of several thousand inhabitants, and early Washingtonians often traveled there to shop for essentials. Commercial activity in Georgetown slumped in the 1820s, with the demise of the tobacco trade and increased competition from port facilities in Alexandria and Washington, but it rebounded with the construction of the Chesapeake and Ohio Canal, begun in 1828. The principal cargo on the canal was coal, but lumber, grain, and limestone for fertilizer were carried as well. The waterfront area filled with wharves, warehouses, factories, and mills. Today the waterfront is dominated by the Whitehurst Freeway, an elevated highway built in 1949. On the left, in the recent view, is the Key Bridge, and beyond it, the spires of Georgetown University.

5 April 1996

c. 1865

Looking north towards Georgetown from Virginia. On the right in the photograph below is the Aqueduct Bridge, constructed between 1833 and 1843. Curiously, the structure supported a water-filled trough, since the bridge was designed to carry canal boats across the river, rather than vehicular traffic. The bridge was part of the Alexandria Canal, a seven-mile waterway that extended the Chesapeake and Ohio Canal south to the port of Alexandria. When this photograph was taken during the Civil War, the bridge was not carrying canal traffic—the aqueduct had been drained and the bridge fitted with a roadbed to carry men and materiel. On the left are four buildings of Georgetown College, founded here in 1789, the first Catholic university in the country. From the left are Gervase (built in the 1830s), Mulledy (1838), Old South (c. 1790, razed 1906), and Maguire (1854). In the recent view, the spires of Healy Hall (construction began in 1879) can be seen. On the banks of the Potomac, below the university, is the Washington Canoe Club, built around 1890.

7 April 1996

1889

Looking south across the Aqueduct Bridge from M Street. The Aqueduct Bridge was not normally so crowded with pedestrians—these people have gathered to see the raging waters of one of Washington's more memorable floods. The 1889 flood submerged Pennsylvania Avenue and the streets of today's Federal Triangle, and devastated the C&O Canal, forcing it into bankruptcy. This photograph shows the Aqueduct Bridge shortly after it was reconstructed; the old wooden superstructure had been demolished and an iron crossing, visible here, was built on the original piers. In the background of the recent photograph is the Key Bridge, completed in 1923. It was constructed alongside the Aqueduct Bridge, which was demolished a decade later. In the foreground of the recent view is a ramp accessing the Whitehurst Freeway, built in 1949.

5 December 1995

23 March 1912

M Street looking southeast from Thirty-sixth Street. In the photograph below, a parade of naval officers, seamen, and marines accompanies the remains of sixty-four unidentified victims of the U.S.S. *Maine* down M Street en route to Arlington Cemetery. The remains were found when the *Maine* was raised from the floor of Havana Harbor in 1912, fourteen years after a mysterious explosion destroyed the ship and killed 266 men. The procession is about to turn left onto the Aqueduct Bridge; the Key Bridge had not yet been built. In the center of the photograph is the one-time home of Francis Scott Key, author of "The Star-Spangled Banner." Key lived here for almost twenty years, until construction of the Chesapeake and Ohio Canal just behind the house drove him to relocate. The house was built around 1802 and at the time of this photograph was open to the public as a museum. Shortly thereafter, it was heavily remodeled, and in 1948 it was razed for construction of a ramp for the Whitehurst Freeway. The ramp itself has since been demolished.

6 April 1996

c. 1910

Looking east on the Chesapeake and Ohio Canal towards the Aqueduct Bridge. Ground was broken for the Chesapeake and Ohio Canal on July 4, 1828. The canal was intended to link Georgetown with Pittsburgh on the Ohio River some 341 miles away. Inspired by the success of the Erie Canal in New York, the canal's backers hoped to bring prosperity to George-town by channeling western trade through the port city. By unhappy coincidence, the cornerstone of the Baltimore and Ohio Railroad was laid in Baltimore that very same day, doom-ing the canal to also-ran status. Construction of the canal continued though, and after many delays it reached Cumberland, Maryland, 184½ miles away, in 1850. With the most

5 December 1995

difficult sections still ahead, construction of the C&O Canal stopped. While rendered obsolete by the railroad, the canal did enjoy a moderate amount of success, peaking in the 1860s and 1870s. In the earlier photograph, canal boats are lined up at Georgetown, waiting their turn to unload. On the right is the towpath where mules, tethered to tow ropes, pulled the canal boats. In the distance is the iron trestle of the Aqueduct Bridge, crossing the canal. In the center of both photographs is the tower of the Capital Traction Company's Union Station, built in 1895 as a streetcar station. In the recent photograph, traffic on Canal Road can be seen on the left. The towpath is now a popular bicycle trail.

c. 1923

Looking west on the Chesapeake and Ohio Canal near Potomac Street. Although competition from the railroads denied the C&O Canal any great measure of success, it remained in operation for almost one hundred years. The demise of the canal finally came in 1924 when it was devastated by a major flood and repairs were deemed impractical. Canal boats, such as the one in this photograph, typically carried a load of 120 tons of coal, grain, or lumber, and were sized to fit the locks with only inches to spare. Just in front of the boat is the water intake of a flour mill. Milling flourished in Georgetown after construction of the canal, with the canal's waters supplying the motive force for the millstones. In 1938 the abandoned canal was purchased by the federal government and it has since been restored as a park.

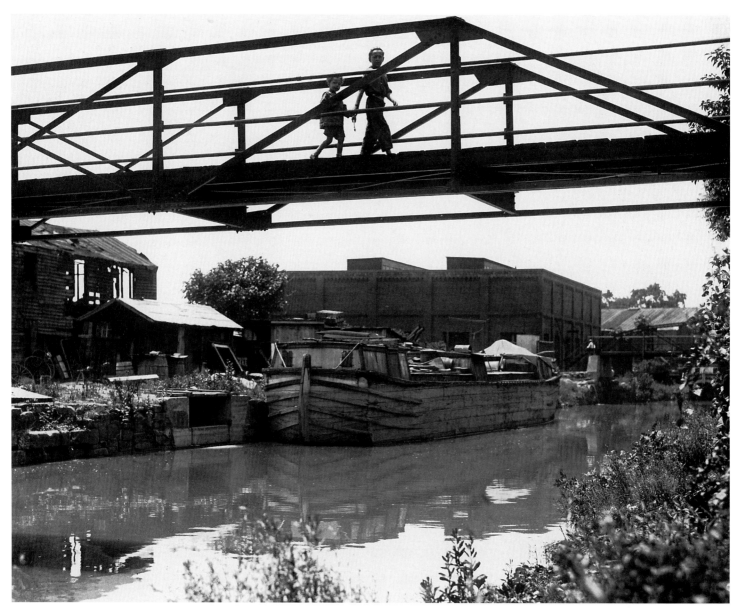

14 October 1995

20 March 1898

Looking south at the 3200 block of M Street. On the right in the recent photograph is Georgetown Park, an upscale shopping mall on M Street just west of Wisconsin Avenue. Built in the 1980s, the mall incorporated the facade of the old M Street shops, a repair facility for streetcars. Washington's first streetcar line, which opened in 1862, ran from this point to the Navy Yard in Southeast Washington. A car barn has occupied this site since that early date, but the age of this structure is not known. Horses pulled the cars until around 1890, when electricity began to take over. Since overhead wires were banned in the area south of Florida Avenue, a method was employed in which the cars were pulled by a cable running in a conduit under the street. The cables were a continuous loop, driven by a wheel in a distant powerhouse. In 1897 the powerhouse at Pennsylvania Avenue and Fourteenth Street (site of the present District Building) burned to the ground, necessitating a brief return to horse power. The photograph below dates from this period. Shortly thereafter, the cables were replaced with underground rails carrying electric current, a system employed for in-town streetcars until they stopped running in 1962.

31 October 1995

1 April 1948

M Street looking west from Wisconsin Avenue. M Street, then as now, was a busy street, lined with shops and restaurants. On the right is the Lido Theatre, which opened in 1909. It closed shortly before this photograph was taken in 1948.

3 January 1996

6 April 1937

Cherry Hill Street (now Cherry Hill Lane) looking east. Alley dwellings were once found all over the city, but these are among the few that have survived. Many did not have indoor plumbing or electricity, and residents generally drew water from a spigot in the backyard, while an outhouse fitted with a barrel accommodated wastes. These houses, built around 1890, were occupied by black families, but other alleys, such as Cecil Place, just to the west of here, were occupied by whites. The photo-

15 December 1995

graph on the left was taken in 1937 by a federal agency empowered to demolish the alleys and replace them with public housing. The houses shown here were renovated, but the vast majority of alley dwellings have since been destroyed. In Southwest Washington, hundreds of such units survived into the 1950s, heated by coal stoves and lit by kerosene lanterns, some only a few blocks from the Capitol. They were razed in the mid-1950s as part of a massive urban renewal project.

Looking northeast at the intersection of Twenty-seventh and Dumbarton streets. In 1937 the area between Twenty-ninth Street and Rock Creek was home to a sizable black community. About one quarter of Georgetown's population was black, as it had been since the early nineteenth century. Long out of fashion as a residential area, Georgetown was in a state of change. In the 1930s young families drawn to Washington by the expansion of the federal government were moving to Georgetown and renovating the old houses there. Over the following decades, the number of black residents fell to a handful, as rising property values forced low-income renters to relocate. The wooden rowhouses on the right in the photograph below were demolished around 1940 and replaced with the present houses, built in brick.

4 October 1995

c. 1925

Looking south towards Rosslyn Circle from the Key Bridge. The photograph below was taken from the foot of the Key Bridge shortly after its completion in 1923. Streetcars from Washington, like the one in the center of the photograph, crossed the new bridge and turned around in Rosslyn Circle. Passengers could walk across the street to the Washington and Old Dominion Railway terminal, the light-colored building on the right. The terminal was opened in 1923 and demolished in 1939. On the left, with a gabled roof, is the terminal of the Washington-Virginia Railway. Passengers could catch trolleys to Mount Vernon on one line, or to Clarendon and Fairfax on another. As late as 1960, Rosslyn looked much as it does in the photograph below. The first office building was completed in 1961, and others followed in rapid succession.

20 April 1996

1922

Lee Highway looking west from Rosslyn Circle. A brewery and a meat-packing plant once occupied the site where the Key Bridge Marriott now stands. The brewery was built in 1896. It was converted to a soda-bottling plant during Prohibition and was demolished in 1958 for construction of the hotel. The railroad tracks are those of the Washington and Old Dominion Railway.

21 March 1996

1922

North Moore Street looking north from Nineteenth Street. Until the raids of 1904, which shutdown many illegal establishments, Rosslyn was a dangerous hell-hole of saloons and gambling dens. By the 1920s the area was a mix of light industry, attracted by the excellent rail connections, and private homes. Later, Rosslyn filled with lumberyards, gas stations, and pawnshops. Overall, it formed a rather seedy gateway to the nation's capital.

15 March 1996

1957

Rosslyn looking north from the Arlington Towers Apartments (now River Place). Change in Rosslyn in the last forty years has been nothing short of astonishing. In 1957 Rosslyn was dominated by businesses supplying the construction industry in the rapidly expanding suburbs. The following year, the Cherry Smash bottling plant, its smokestack visible to the rear in the photograph below, was demolished for the construction of the Marriott hotel. In 1961 Rosslyn's first office building was completed. Today, Tom Saris's restaurant, in 1957 an electronics store, stands surrounded by giants, the sole reminder of Rosslyn's past.

22 October 1996

c. 1918

Wilson Boulevard looking east from Washington Boulevard. Clarendon began life as a streetcar suburb, laid out as a subdivision at the turn of the century along the trolley tracks, which reached the area in 1897. In the photograph below, a trolley car of the Washington-Virginia Railway is stopped at Clarendon station on its way to Fairfax. The station was built in 1904 and demolished in 1922 for the construction of a bank. With competition from automobiles, Northern Virginia's trolleys struggled through the 1920s and finally died in 1939. The bank was razed in 1974, and today a war memorial occupies the site.

1 March 1996

c. 1936

Wilson Boulevard looking northeast from Irving Street. In the 1930s Clarendon was Arlington's downtown. In the era before shopping malls, this block of Wilson Boulevard resembled the main street of a small town, with drug stores, restaurants, a bowling alley, and a theater. The block on the right in the photograph below was demolished in 1974 for the construction of the Clarendon Metro station. After the station was completed a number of ethnic restaurants were established here, and for a time Clarendon was the commercial center of the area's Vietnamese community.

15 March 1996

c. 1894

Lee Highway looking southwest towards the East Falls Church railroad station. In the photograph below, a muddy Lee Highway leads past the railroad station (center, to the right of Lee Highway) and on towards Falls Church. The photograph was taken by a member of the Eastman family, which occupied a house outside the frame on the right, behind the picket fence. The house remained in the family until 1995 when the last family member died. It now stands surrounded by a townhouse development.

25 January 1996

1898

Looking southeast towards Lee Highway. In the photograph below, taxis congregate at the trolley station, waiting to ferry soldiers and visitors to Camp Russell A. Alger, a training camp for the Spanish-American War. Camp Alger lay several miles away, near the present-day intersection of the Capital Beltway and Route 50. The trolley line, then known as the Washington, Arlington and Falls Church Railway, terminated at this station.

21 March 1996

c. 1920

Looking northwest towards Lee Highway from Fairfax Drive. Northern Virginia was still rural when the photograph below was taken around 1920. On the left is the East Falls Church Station of the Washington and Old Dominion Railway. The station was dismantled after the railroad closed in 1968, and the right-of-way has since become a bicycle path. In the center of the photograph is Elliot's hardware store, built in 1903. Later Snyder and Company hardware, it burned in 1948 and was rebuilt at the same location. Snyder's closed in 1996.

5 March 1996

c. 1890

The intersection of Broad Street (Route 7) and Washington Street (Route 29) looking north. Brown's Hardware opened as a general store in 1883 and is now run by the grandson of the original owner. The building in the photograph below was demolished in 1959, doomed by the widening of North Washington Street, on the right. It was replaced by the present structure, part of which is visible on the left in the recent view.

25 January 1996

c. 1950

The intersection of Broad Street (Route 7) and Washington Street (Route 29) looking south. At the time of the photograph below, before suburban sprawl, Falls Church was one of the most important commercial centers in Northern Virginia. Route 7 had just been widened, in 1947, from a shady two-lane strip only twenty-four feet wide, to four lanes. The gas station on the corner was built in the 1920s and demolished in 1963 for the widening of Washington Street (foreground). The lot was vacant for many years until Independence Square, on the left in the recent photograph, was completed in 1985.

2 February 1996

c. 1935

Looking west towards the intersection of Route 7 and Route 123. On the right in the photograph below, facing Route 7 (running left-right), is the Tyson's Corner Store, once the property of William Tyson. In 1902 it was acquired by Samuel and Savilla Myers and operated by their family for many years. On the left is the Cross Roads Market. The two stores stood in what is now the median strip of Route 7, and both were demolished in 1964 when the thoroughfare was expanded to four lanes. Route 123 can be seen winding its way off through farmland towards Vienna. In 1964 it was relocated somewhat to the northwest (to the right in these photographs).

5 March 1996

1956

Looking southeast towards the Cross Roads Market. In 1954 Tysons Corner was still a rural crossroads, although suburban subdivisions were starting to encroach on the area. The Cross Roads Market stood at the corner of Route 123 (foreground), and Route 7 (to the left). The widening of Route 7 in 1964 necessitated destruction of the building, for it would have stood directly in the median of the new thoroughfare. The interchange between Route 7 and Route 123 was built that same year. It lies behind the camera position in the recent photograph.

29 March 1997

c. 1903

Main Street looking east from Chain Bridge Road. In 1800 the Fairfax County courthouse was moved to this crossroads from Alexandria, after that city was incorporated into the new District of Columbia. In the following decades, a town grew up around the new courthouse. After the Civil War the town had stagnated, primarily due to its isolation. The county's roads were often impassable in bad weather, and the nearest rail stop was at Fairfax Station, several miles to the south. In 1904 a trolley line reached the village from Washington, and the town finally began to grow, now as a suburb of the capital city.

March 1996

c. 1910

Looking southeast towards Herndon Station. Herndon grew up around the railroad, which first reached the area around 1856. Fairfax County farms supplied dairy products to Washington, and Herndon station became an important shipping point. The railroad also provided access to commuters. As early as the late nineteenth century a number of government workers lived in Herndon and commuted to Washington by train.

16 November 1995

c. 1910

Looking northwest towards Herndon Station. The rail line that ran through Herndon led from Alexandria westward to Bluemont at the base of the Blue Ridge. The line was begun before the Civil War as a competitor for the Baltimore and Ohio Railroad, but funds were short and it was never completed. Instead, it survived as a local carrier, principally hauling agricultural produce. By the time of the photograph below, the line was a branch of the Southern Railway. Shortly thereafter, in 1911, the line was incorporated into the newly formed Washington and Old Dominion Railway and converted from steam to electric power. The last passenger train ran in 1951, but freight service continued until the line closed in 1968.

8 April 1997

1928

Looking north on Washington Street towards the intersection with King Street. Despite the similar appearance of these two views, the only building shown below and still standing in the recent photograph is the one on the right corner, built around 1800. The federal-style building on the left corner was demol- ished in the 1950s and replaced with a colonial revival struc- ture. The city of Alexandria is in fact older than either Wash- ington or Georgetown. A tobacco warehouse was built on the site around 1740, and in 1749 the town was laid out and the first lots sold.

21 December 1995

c. 1907

Looking east on King Street towards the intersection with Pitt Street. On the right in the earlier view is the Marshall House hotel, built around 1785. When Virginia seceded from the Union in 1861, the defiant proprietor, James W. Jackson, flew the Confederate flag from the hotel, declaring that it would be removed over his dead body. When federal troops invaded the city on May 24 of that year, Colonel Elmer Ellsworth of New York spotted the flag and tore it down. As he was descending the stairs, Jackson shot him and was himself immediately killed by Corporal Francis Brownell. Ellsworth was the first Union officer killed in the war; Jackson achieved martyrdom; and Brownell was awarded the medal of honor for his efforts. The much-altered Marshall House was razed in 1951 for the construction of a Virginia state liquor store, itself demolished in the mid-1960s for an urban renewal project. The Holiday Inn was built on the site in the 1970s.

30 January 1996

November 1962

Looking northeast towards the 700 block of King Street.
These four townhouses were probably built around 1816. They have served a number of uses since. The building that housed Brown's Men's Shop in 1962 was converted from a residence to a store in 1912. It is now the home of Murphy's Irish pub.

8 March 1997

August 1862

Looking northeast towards the 1300 block of Duke Street. The main building of a large slave dealership is still standing at 1315 Duke Street. While the present building once housed offices for clerks and overseers, another around the corner, now gone, served as a barracks for the slaves. Slaves were bought and sold here, and there were quarters for visiting plantation owners. After Union troops seized the city, the compound was used as a military prison, at which time the photograph below was taken. Number 1315 Duke Street, much altered, today houses the offices of the Northern Virginia Urban League.

21 December 1995

1923

The 1500 block of Duke Street looking east from Dainger-field Road. In the fifty years since the earlier photograph was taken, Duke Street has been widened from two lanes to five.

Hooffs Run, once a health hazard, now flows through a culvert. The Shiloh Baptist Church is still standing, visible in the center of each photograph. It was built in 1891.

29 January 1996

c. 1947

Wisconsin Avenue looking north from Western Avenue. Commercial development has grown tremendously on this stretch of Wisconsin Avenue in the fifty years that separate these two photographs. On the left, single-family houses can be seen where an office building now stands. On the right, behind the stone monument, is a newly constructed Howard Johnson's restaurant. The monument, installed in 1932, marks the state boundary. At some point in the intervening five decades, it was rotated 180 degrees, and now welcomes Maryland-bound motorists with the words "District of Columbia."

10 March 1997

c. 1915

Looking north towards the intersection of Wisconsin Avenue and Old Georgetown Road. When the photograph below was taken, around 1915, farming had largely disappeared in Bethesda and much of the land was in the hands of investors and developers. A number of subdivisions were laid out in the area starting in the 1890s, but by 1915 few of the lots had been sold. The building on the left is a gatehouse for the Edgewood subdivision, later renamed Edgemoor. In 1919 the building became the first home of the Bank of Bethesda. The bank later moved to the stone building in the center of the recent photograph, now occupied by a branch of Crestar Bank. The trolley tracks were laid down in 1891 and continued on to Rockville. The trolleys stopped running in 1935.

20 June 1996

c. 1915

Connecticut Avenue looking north from Bradley Lane. When the first resident moved to Chevy Chase in 1893, the new subdivision was five miles from Washington, surrounded by countryside. The development was the work of Francis Newlands, a wealthy lawyer and mining heir from Nevada, who later served as congressman and senator. Beginning in the late 1880s Newlands bought up land along the path of today's Connecticut Avenue from Rock Creek almost to the present-day Capital Beltway. To provide access to his subdivision, Newlands (and other investors) paid for the construction of Connecticut Avenue and the adjacent trolley line. Sales of lots were slowed by the Panic of 1893, however, and didn't really take off until after World War I. Nevertheless, Newland's Chevy Chase Land Company survived, backed by his tremendous wealth, and remains in business today. The trolley line, visible in the photograph below, was closed in 1935.

21 March 1996

c. 1910

Connecticut Avenue looking north from Rock Creek. In the era before automobiles became the dominant means of transportation, this section of Connecticut Avenue north of Chevy Chase (and today's Capital Beltway) was a rural byway rather than the important thoroughfare it is today. Real estate salesmen were early and enthusiastic motorists, for a thrilling ride in the country helped convince prospective homeowners of the joys of suburban living.

31 March 1996

1918

Rockville Pike looking north from Grosvenor Lane. In the photograph below, men and women work together spreading asphalt on Rockville Pike during World War I. The use of female labor was necessitated by a wartime labor shortage. The street sign in the center of the photograph reads "Grosvenor Lane." To the left lay the estate of Gilbert H. Grosvenor, president of the National Geographic Society. A number of such estates were scattered across suburban Maryland, at the time still quite rural.

30 June 1996

1917

East Montgomery Avenue looking southeast. Rockville probably dates from the 1750s, when it began as a way station along the road between Georgetown and Frederick. The first lots were laid out in the 1780s, and suburban growth began in 1873 when a new branch of the Baltimore and Ohio Railroad connected the town with Washington. In the photograph below, East Montgomery Avenue leads east through Rockville's commercial center. The trolley tracks, laid down in 1900, carried commuters to Washington. East Montgomery Avenue itself no longer exists; it was eliminated in the 1960s in an urban renewal project that transformed the city center. The project demolished 111 buildings covering forty-six acres and housing over 150 businesses. Replacing them was Rockville Mall, which opened in 1972 with only ten stores! Razed in 1995, the mall occupied the now-vacant site to the left in the recent photograph. More successful were an apartment complex constructed in 1974 (not visible here), and two county office buildings (center and right in the recent view) built in the 1980s. Currently, the city plans to reconfigure the site yet again, restoring the streets and shops that were demolished in the 1960s, albeit in a different form.

13 March 1996

c. 1954

East Montgomery Avenue looking northwest. By the late 1950s downtown Rockville presented a motley appearance to the eyes of city officials. Business was starting to suffer from competition from new malls such as Congressional Plaza, and shoppers complained about traffic and a lack of parking. Many of the buildings were old residences with added store-fronts, and some were in poor condition. In 1960 an urban renewal plan was approved. Five years later, after many delays, the mayor kicked off demolition of the city center by pitching a rock through the window of a Civil War–era house. Bulldozers quickly finished the job. Within a few years, East Montgomery Avenue had ceased to exist. In the center of the photograph below is the tower of the old Montgomery County Courthouse, built in 1891. Spared during urban renewal, it is still standing today. Filling the present view is the Montgomery County Executive Office Building.

20 March 1996

Georgia Avenue looking south towards Silver Spring Avenue. Although it was served by the Baltimore and Ohio Railroad and a trolley line, Silver Spring was bypassed in the first round of suburban development that began in the 1880s. It wasn't until the 1920s that the first subdivision was laid out in the area. When the photograph below was taken in 1917, Silver Spring was still a sleepy village. Many of the buildings in this view are still standing. The Silver Spring Armory, in the center of the photograph, was acquired by the Silver Spring Fire Department in 1919. Now sporting a colonial revival facade, the building is still used as a firehouse.

19 March 1996

c. 1910

Baltimore Avenue (Route 1) looking north from the 5100 block. Hyattsville grew up in the mid-nineteenth century where the B&O Railroad crossed the Washington and Baltimore Turnpike (now Route 1). In 1873 the first suburban subdivision in this part of Prince Georges County was laid out at Hyattsville. Suburban growth really took off after 1899, when the trolley tracks, visible in the foreground, reached the town. By 1950 Prince Georges County had grown tremendously, and the strip along Route 1 was the county's commercial center. With the rise of suburban shopping malls in the following decades, Hyattsville began to fade.

6 January 1996

c. 1910

Baltimore Avenue (Route 1) looking north from the University of Maryland. Before the B&O Railroad was constructed through the area in 1835, the Washington and Baltimore Turnpike was the main route between the two cities. The building in the center of each photograph, the Rossborough Inn, was built in 1803 and served weary travelers along the pike. When the photograph below was taken around 1910, the trolley and railroad lines that paralleled the pike to the east carried most of the traffic through the area. With the rise of the automobile, the turnpike, now Route 1, again became a major thoroughfare.

13 January 1996

c. 1936

Looking east towards the 7400 block of Baltimore Avenue (Route 1). As the federal government expanded in the 1930s, the suburbs in Prince Georges County grew dramatically.

Commercial development, once centered along the trolley tracks, now spread to Route 1, as the automobile made more of the county accessible.

6 January 1996

September 1937

The old Berwyn Post Office looking northwest from Berwyn Road. There was once a thriving commercial district in Berwyn where the trolley tracks crossed Berwyn Road. The trolleys ran through here until 1958, and the right-of-way can still be seen. The two men in the foreground are probably waiting for a Washington-bound trolley.

31 January 1996

PHOTOGRAPH CREDITS